SIXTY SHADES
OF SUNDAY

INVESTMENT THOUGHTS

JOHN LOOBY

Published by Oak Tree Press, 19 Rutland Street, Cork, Ireland.
www.oaktreepress.com / www.SuccessStore.com

ISBN: 978-1-78119-190 -3 (paperback)

Cover image by JustASC / 123RF Stock Photo.

Cover design by Kieran O'Connor Design.

Printed in Ireland by SPRINT-print Ltd.

CONTENTS

DEDICATION

To my family, for making it all possible and giving it all meaning.

ACKNOWLEDGEMENTS

I would like to thank *The Sunday Times, The Sunday Business Post, The Sunday Tribune, Business & Finance, The Irish Times* and The Value Investment Institute for publishing these pieces originally.

INTRODUCTION

The dominant orthodoxy in finance over the past 60 years has been the Efficient Markets Hypothesis (EMH). Developed by a varied group of US academics from the early 1950s, some of whom subsequently received Nobel prizes for their efforts, the key conclusion of this orthodoxy is that trying to beat financial markets is a fool's errand. In a process analogous to Brownian motion, market prices jiggle about randomly, discounting all new information in an all but instantaneous fashion, thereby rendering it impossible to beat the market.

In the face of this conclusion, the rational investor should eschew any attempt to try and beat the market and should gain their exposure *via* relatively low-cost passive vehicles. The explosive growth of such vehicles, pioneered by John Bogle at Vanguard in the US in the early 1970s and subsequently spread across the financial world, is testament to the powerful and enduring influence of the EMH.

Despite this success and the plausible reasoning underpinning it, the EMH has shown sufficient flaws to suggest that the attempt to beat the market may not always be a foolhardy endeavour. There are inefficiencies in the behaviour of market economies and the financial markets embedded within them, which the active investor with the right approach has an attractive probability of exploiting. If successful, the rewards can be substantial.

Of course that is not to say that the market is easy to beat, or in the saltier words of Charlie Munger, the long-time business partner of Warren Buffett at Berkshire Hathaway:

> "It's not supposed to be easy. Anyone who finds it easy is stupid".

I have spent the past 25 years trying not to be stupid. More recently, I've shared thoughts on this goal in regular newspaper opinion pieces.

With the challenge of beating the market as daunting as ever, I thought it timely to bring these pieces together in a new collection. I hope you enjoy it. But more importantly, as you navigate your own investment journey, I hope you find something of interest here.

Good luck.

John Looby
January 2015

1: HISTORY TEACHES THERE'S NO AVOIDING BUBBLE TROUBLE

The Sunday Times, 3 October 2010

With debate in Ireland becoming more rancorous about the state of the economy and the public finances, it seems timely to place our current travails in a different context.

A cursory glance at history shows that the extraordinary economic progress of much of the globe since the late 18th century has been occasionally reversed and temporarily silenced by the sound of a loudly-bursting asset-price bubble.

Within the past 15 years alone, the global economy has been rocked by three such episodes: the 'Asian Crisis', the 'Dot-Com Collapse', and the 'Credit Crisis'. They have caused widespread economic dislocation amid financial market turmoil. Coming hard on the heels of the 'Nikkei Collapse' and the 'Latin-American Debt Crisis', which erupted in the previous two decades, this trinity of asset-price devastation should serve again to underline how rapidly-rising and chaotically-collapsing asset prices are by no means unusual.

The painful bursting of our own version of an asset-price bubble (property), while clearly containing many important lessons for domestic players, needs to be seen and understood in this broader sense.

The evolution of the global financial and banking system since medieval Europe is the crucial enabler of this process. Simply put, as long as the banking system is allowed to borrow on a short-term basis from depositors who effectively are taxpayer-guaranteed, and lend on a long-term basis for investments with an uncertain outcome, cycles of excessive exuberance and depression are inevitable.

A key implication of this is that asset markets are in a constant process of movement towards, or arrival at, an excessively exuberant or depressed state – that is, a *bubble*. There is nothing about our current predicament in Ireland and how we got here that can't be understood against this broad backdrop.

Equally, those in the political, regulatory and media world charged with explaining or addressing the drama of the last three years, in generally well-intentioned and probably socially-necessary investigations, are as unlikely to produce lasting, relevant change as their many predecessors.

Certainly better regulation, less reckless bank lending and more sober borrowing behaviour are all to be commended, but this genie can't be returned to the bottle.

Just look at the gyrations of the Chinese stock market, the oil price, or the bonds issued by US corporations over the past two years. It is clear that the outlook for the Chinese economy, the likely demand/supply evolution for crude oil, or the changing default probability of corporate America, struggle to credibly account for the inflating exuberance or deflating depression of such dramatic price movements.

The inconvenient truth is that asset markets have an ongoing tendency towards the inflating or deflating of price bubbles.

In attempting to identify future bubbles, it may be worthwhile to consider the following:

- Global interest rates are at multi-decade lows;
- The global monetary base (effectively, the cash available to circulate) is at a multi-decade high;
- Developed-world government borrowing is at a peace-time high.

These dramatic policy responses to the post-Lehman financial market and economic earthquake now may be furnishing the raw material for future dramatic asset-price behaviour.

In particular, the possibilities that such cheap and abundantly available 'paper' may be *dangerously* channelled by the financial and banking system into 'the next big thing', or that the withdrawal of such availability may prompt a fresh and disorderly general flight from 'risk' (for example, stocks, commodities and property) now must be highlighted.

Where will this excessively exuberant or depressed asset-price movement take place next? The answer is that nobody can know for sure. The relative valuation case generally supporting equities may suggest 'not here', while the recent accelerated fall in the sovereign bond yields (borrowing costs) of the US, the UK and Germany, for example, may prove a more likely candidate. Unfortunately though, the past experience and future certainty of asset-price bubbles offers little (if any) insight into where or when such bubbles will occur next.

In the face of this uncertainty, investor seat-belts can do little better than being always buckled by *sufficient* diversification and *sensible* asset valuation. The avoidance of any investment requiring a 'this time it is different' rationale should be a golden rule of thumb in this respect – bubbles may be inevitable, but losing money when they burst doesn't have to be.

The policy-maker version of the above advice, meanwhile, points strongly to the need for the State always to minimise long-term fixed commitments that suddenly may become unaffordable. The failure to understand this in Ireland has left us with our current excessive dependence on the goodwill of potentially fickle lenders. Only by grasping this soon can we hope to remain authors of our own economic future.

2: A POLITICAL CASE FOR IRISH BONDS

The Sunday Business Post, 17 October 2010

The now infamous words of Bill Clinton's advisor, James Carville, have echoed loudly around Ireland in recent months:

> "I used to think if there was reincarnation, I wanted to come back as the President or the Pope or a .400 baseball hitter. But now I want to come back as the bond market. You can intimidate everybody".

Instead of delving into the minutiae of bank rescue costs, fiscal retrenchment choices or the machinations of bond traders and the ECB, I want to make a case for Irish bonds that rests on the politics of our position. After all, it was political choices that have resulted in the current crisis, and it will be the political decisions made here and in the EU that will determine its outcome.

I believe that there will be no default of Irish sovereign debt. Irish 15-year bonds currently offering an annual return of over 6.5% are a compelling investment.

The reason why I make such a statement with what many may feel is foolhardy conviction is that when I ask the central question: "What does the European Union want?", it is the only conclusion which makes sense.

Fundamentally, a union that has evolved from the rubble of 1945 to be in the process of taking its chair at the top-table of the evolving multi-polar world is not going to be undone by failing to address the debt problems of a minor, or for that matter any, member state.

A potpourri of randomly-chosen recent stories from around the world give some impression of the likely multi-polar future that is now emerging and the jockeying for position that is underway:

- Within weeks of taking office, US Secretary of State Clinton and Treasury Secretary Geithner were in Beijing;

- The decision of the US to withdraw combat troops from Iraq has prompted a massive arms order for US firms from Saudi Arabia and its fellow Gulf States;

- British Conservative Prime Minister Cameron grows in resolve to back his deficit-cutting Chancellor over the spending ambitions of his Defence Secretary;

- Brazilian Finance Minister Mantega makes global headlines with mention of an 'international currency war';

- The EU and South Korea sign one of the largest bilateral trade deals in history.

Against this emerging reality, the leadership of the EU and its larger member states can't but be aware that a strong and stable union (and currency) is their only route to long-term influence in a rapidly-evolving world order.

This lesson is clearly understood across the Atlantic. In the wake of the collapse of Lehman Brothers in September 2008, the US economy and banking system faced collapse. The scale of 'bad debt' throughout its traumatised financial system seemed likely to overwhelm it, and to undermine significantly the leading position of the United States in the world. This view failed to reckon with the powerful levers available to US policy-makers that were used as the over-arching political imperative of safeguarding US relative power trumped everything else.

Of most relevance, the Federal Reserve (the US Central Bank) embarked upon a determined policy of purchasing large quantities of distressed mortgage-backed securities, US Treasury Bonds and other assets – effectively with dollars it printed for this purpose. In effect, it took on the role of an enormous NAMA, with the important difference that it paid for the assets it bought with money it printed rather than borrowed. Though unconventional and risky, the goal of protecting the US in the global pecking order was just too important to be left to orthodoxy and market forces.

The tragic German experience with hyperinflation in the 1920s, which has been so central in informing Bundesbank, and subsequently

European Central Bank, thinking about monetary policy, clearly suggests that any equivalent move within the Euro-zone will not be enacted lightly. The continuing reluctance of the ECB to resort to the 'printing presses' in the face of the problems in Greece, and now Ireland, underlines this reality.

In any case, such a question may never arise. If the Irish state decides to go down the road of walking away from some of its liabilities, it will begin/continue in the following order:

- Capital projects (no Dublin Metro, etc.);
- Public sector wages (Croke Park deal is re-structured);
- Welfare costs (rationalised down towards UK levels);
- Bank sub-debt holders;
- Recourse to the Greek-style IMF/ECB/EU support mechanism;
- Haircut for depositors/senior bond holders;
- Haircut for Irish government bond holders.

Ultimately, however, the global political ambitions of the EU will not be stymied by a Bundesbank-adhering ECB, and the last two stages above will never be reached. The ultimate prize is just too big.

3: GLOBAL LENDING IMBALANCE MAKES EQUITIES ATTRACTIVE

The Sunday Times, 31 October 2010

Ben Graham, the man whom the most successful investor in history, Warren Buffett, credits as his teacher and inspiration, once summarised his deceptively simple approach to investment:

> "The only (investment) principle that has ever worked well consistently is to buy common stocks at such times as they are cheap by analysis, and to sell them at such times as they are dear by analysis. That sounds like timing; but it is not really timing at all but rather the purchase and sale of securities by the method of valuation".

In contrast to a conventional attempt to pronounce on the outlook for economic growth, future inflation or interest rates, or indeed to offer an analysis derived from balance sheets, income and cash-flow statements, I want to make a case for equities based on a simple story of how the growing payments imbalance between the developed world (largely, the United States) and the developing world (largely, China) has driven the valuation of equities into strikingly attractive territory.

As recently as 15 years ago, the global economy was in broad balance, with consumers and governments in the developed and developing world broadly consuming the value of their own output. Since then, this position has changed dramatically, as consumers and governments in the developed world have been consuming vastly more than the value of their output and their counterparts in the developing world have been doing the mirror opposite. With many developing countries effectively determined to maintain fixed exchange rates *versus* the US dollar, the resulting flow has seen a large and quickening movement of capital from the developing world (especially, China) to the developed world (especially, the US).

The key question for this story is: "Where has this capital been flowing?".

The sharp decline in the bond yields (government interest rates) of the US, the UK and Germany to their current multi-decade lows has had many drivers. Investor fear, historically-low official interest rates and subdued inflation expectations are just three of the many often cited. However, the huge flow of developing world capital into the bond markets of these developed world countries also must be playing a significant role.

For example, China was a negligible holder of US government bonds as recently as 10 years ago, but is today the biggest private lender to the US Government. This scale of capital flow from China into US Treasuries, and more generally from the developing world to the government bond markets of the developed world, certainly must be contributing to the dramatic plummeting of their bond yields.

Simply put, the growing savings of the developing world largely are being loaned by their governments, at lower and lower interest rates, to satisfy the growing borrowing demands of their developed world counterparts. President Obama, Chancellor Merkel and Prime Minister Cameron all are borrowing now at a 10-year interest rate of under 2.5% – less than half the rate their predecessors faced a decade ago.

By contrast, consider the earnings yield (interest rate) currently offered by a selection of globally-recognised companies across a broad spectrum of economic activity:

- Pfizer: 11%;
- Nestlé: 6.6%;
- Diageo: 7%;
- Vodafone: 10.8%;
- Nike: 5%;
- Exxon Mobil: 6.1%;
- Microsoft: 9.3%;
- CRH: 6.5%;

- Intel: 10.1%;
- Johnson and Johnson: 7%.

While many may argue that I should cite dividend rather than earnings yields, or cash-flow-based returns rather than earnings-based ones, or eschew both in favour of analysing balance sheets, the key point is that many financially-sound, competitively well-positioned, globally-recognised companies are currently offering an 'interest rate', however defined, substantially higher than that being offered by developed world government bond markets.

The savings of the developing world, largely directed by their governments, is spurning the value in equities such as these, in favour of developed world bond markets offering historically low returns. This is not sustainable.

It seems safe to assume that this is the kind of value opportunity that would have appealed greatly to Ben Graham and it is no surprise that his greatest student, speaking earlier this month at a conference hosted by *Fortune* magazine, said:

"I can't imagine anybody having bonds in their portfolio when they can own equities. But that's what makes for the attractive prices".

4: WHAT DOES 'ECONOMIC GOODWILL' MEAN FOR THE VALUE INVESTOR?

Value Investment Institute, November 2010

When the father of value investing, Ben Graham, formalised his approach with David Dodd in the now iconic book *Security Analysis* in 1934, he made clear his goal of buying stocks at a discount to their net current assets (cash and other assets that can be turned into cash within one year, such as accounts receivable and inventory, less all liabilities).

In advocating this famous Net/Net approach to stock investing, Graham was attaching little or no value to any long-term tangible assets that a firm may possess. For many who studied and ultimately followed Graham, the extreme conservatism of such an approach became increasingly questionable as they grew comfortable in their ability to assign a value to long-term tangible assets such as Property, Plant and Equipment.

As the memory of the Great Depression faded, the market began to re-rate upwards in the 1950s and 1960s, leaving fewer Net/Net stocks on offer to investors. Investors such as the legendary Walter Schloss broadened the search for cheap stocks to buying stocks at a discount to their net tangible assets. Although a less conservative approach than Net/Net, this liquidation valuation approach (where only tangible assets are assigned a value) subsequently has been viewed as overly restrictive. In particular, it lacks the critical insight that many value investors bring to the discipline, including the most successful and well-known value investor of them all, Warren Buffett.

The argument that there may be significant value lurking and worth paying for in something Buffett calls 'economic goodwill', which holds little weight for Schloss and arguably held even less for Graham, is a central tenet of the Buffett approach to stock investing. Indeed, given what we know about some of his most successful stock investments (their purchase at a substantial *premium* to net tangible assets), it is no exaggeration to suggest that his extraordinary investment success would not have been possible without this crucial insight.

He succinctly summarised his thinking on this issue in his 1983 letter to shareholders of Berkshire Hathaway:

> "Businesses logically are worth far more than net tangible assets when they can be expected to produce earnings on such assets considerably in excess of market rates of return. The capitalised value of this excess return is Economic Goodwill".

Of particular practical significance, this insight of Buffett frees the investor to largely by-pass the often thorny issues surrounding accounting goodwill. Questions such as whether goodwill is being fairly valued on the balance sheet by management or, more fundamentally, its definitional failure to capture potentially important assets such as intellectual property effectively can be left to one side, as the investor seeks to value the business in its entirety – its net asset value, as an asset generating 'market rates of return'.

For such an investor, the business is worth the sum of its net tangible assets and 'economic goodwill'. The goal of a value investor such as Buffett is to buy stocks at a discount to this valuation.

To consider how this approach may be applied, the following example under the following assumptions may be helpful:

- Total Tangible Assets are assumed to equal the sum of 'Total Current Assets', 'Long-Term Assets', 'Net Fixed Assets', 'Investments in Associated Companies' and 'Other Long-Term Assets' on the balance sheet below.

- Net Tangible Assets is the net of Total Tangible Assets and Total Liabilities.

- Net Profit is assumed to equate to the Buffett definition quoted earlier of earnings that the business 'can be expected to produce'.

Vodafone - Balance Sheet: March 2010

Assets

Cash & Near-Term Cash	745
Other Short-Term Investments	4,066
Accounts Receivable	4,008
Inventories	433
Other Current Assets	2,136
Total Current Assets	11,388
Long-Term Investments	7,650
Net Fixed Assets	20,642
Net Intangible Assets	74,258
Investments in Associated Companies	36,377
Other Long-Term Assets	6,670
Total Long-Term Assets	145,597
Total Assets	156,985
Total Tangible Assets	82,727

Liabilities

Accounts Payable	3,254
Short-Term Borrowings	11,184
Other Short-Term liabilities	14,178
Total Current Liabilities	28,616
Long-Term Borrowings	28,686
Other Long-Term Liabilities	8,873
Total Long-Term Liabilities	37,559
Total Liabilities	66,175
Net Tangible Assets	16,552
Net Profit	8,645
Return on Net Tangible Assets	52.23

Applying these assumptions, this is a business that is generating a return on net tangible assets of over 52%. Again, to quote Buffett, a return considerably greater than 'market rates of return'.

Making the further assumption, that with 10-Year UK gilts currently yielding below 3.5% and that adding a 'risk premium' of over 5% to this 'risk-free' rate is ample, the reasonable required rate of return for this investment (again, in Buffett terms, 'market rates of return') is assumed to be 8.5%.

A value can now be assigned to the 'Economic Goodwill' and consequently the entirety of this business i.e. its Net Asset Value, to a value investor such as Buffett.

Net Tangible Assets	16,522
Economic Goodwill	85,148
Required Return	8.5
Net Asset Value	101,700

The current market capitalisation (the net asset value assigned to this business by the stock-market) is 75,368 (8 July 2010). Thus, in this illustration and under the assumptions made, the discount to its net asset value (101,700) which this business is on offer for is just shy of 26%; a margin of safety likely sufficient for many a value investor to take a position.

While paying due homage therefore to the ground-breaking work of Graham and the many who have strictly followed his approach with great success, it seems nonetheless clear that the importance of 'economic goodwill' to value investing, largely ignored by Graham but introduced by his most famous student, Buffett, can often be central.

5: RISK IS UNAVOIDABLE WITH INVESTMENT IN BANKS

The Sunday Business Post, 28 November 2010

From well-known broadcasters and politicians to unknown strangers and (some) friends, the anecdotal list of those who have lost significant sums investing in Irish bank shares seems to be a long one. A recent story in the property supplement of *The Irish Times* made for particularly sober reading:

> "George Stevens of the well-known Bray-based firm GA Stevens & Son doesn't just move people, he listens to their woes too, it seems.
>
> "A lot of our customers are destroyed, people who would have always been rock solid. We have customers, a couple, who were downsizing and sold their house before the crash and decided to rent for a while to see how they liked apartment living. They invested €1.7 million in bank shares with four different banks and their life savings ended up being worth only €59,000. That's happened to a lot of people and they certainly couldn't be blamed for being greedy'".

While, hopefully, this is one of the more extreme cases of financial loss suffered, it underlines starkly the unavoidable risk and potential loss that is always involved in owning shares in a bank – a risk as relevant and unchanging for any investor in any bank share at any time, as it unfortunately has proven for the customers of George Stevens and many other investors in Irish bank shares in recent times.

The fact that so many of these investors seem to have sunk most, if not all, of their wealth into Irish bank shares suggests that the nature of this risk is poorly understood. I can't be sure whether this is because the majority were mistakenly conflating investing in the shares of a bank with saving in a deposit account with a bank, or were just swept along by the excitement of rapidly-rising share prices, but it seems clear, at a minimum, that they were insufficiently aware of their exposure to the risk of such significant losses.

In order to understand the nature of this risk, there is no reason to become mired in a turgid discussion about capital ratios, bond categories or any of the other distracting terms that seem to have been clogging much of our media in recent times. Instead, I believe a simple example of how a new bank – let's call it XBank – is financed and operates will make clear the nature of the unavoidable risk and potential loss that is always involved in investing in the shares of a bank.

For simplicity, let's assume that:

- The only capital of XBank is that provided by its shareholders – there is no subordinated debt;

- The only borrowing of XBank is that provided by its depositors – there is no senior debt;

- The only assets of XBank are the loans it makes to its borrowers – there is no holding of cash or near-cash reserves;

- The regulatory capital buffer of XBank is 5% of its assets.

On the basis of the above, let's now assume that XBank raises €5 in capital from shareholders when it is floated on the market. With this €5 capital buffer in place, XBank now borrows €95 from its depositors and loans €100 to its borrowers. Its profit is generated by the interest rate difference between what it pays on its borrowings to its depositors and what it receives on its loans from its borrowers.

In summary, the balance sheet of XBank looks like this:

XBank – Balance Sheet

Assets €		Liabilities €	
Loans	100	Deposits	95
		Shareholder Capital	5
Total	**100**	**Total**	**100**

Now consider a scenario where some of those who have borrowed from XBank are unable to repay part of their borrowing. More specifically, consider the scenario where just 5% of the borrowing from XBank is not repaid – in other words, XBank suffers a loss of €5 (for real-world comparison purposes, recall that the equivalent loss in Anglo-Irish Bank is currently projected to be an almost incomprehensible 40%). As losses are borne by the shareholders, in this scenario where 95% of the loans made by XBank are repaid, the shareholders nonetheless will lose their entire investment.

This is the key message: due to the necessarily leveraged nature of how any bank is financed and operates, relatively small losses (falls in its assets/failure of its borrowers to repay) can have a devastating effect on the value of shareholder investment.

While clearly there have been times, and may well be times in the future, when bank share prices rise, the next time that a friendly stockbroker or financial advisor recommends that you invest in a bank share I recommend that you tell the story of XBank.

If that isn't sufficient to change the subject, you might finally consider quoting the maestro himself, Alan Greenspan, from October 2008:

> "Those of us who have looked to the self-interest of lending institutions (banks) to protect shareholder's equity – myself especially – are in a state of shocked disbelief".

6: LATVIA HAS SHOWN THAT DEBT DEFAULT IS NOT THE ONLY ANSWER

The Sunday Tribune, 9 January 2011

The list of domestic and international commentators arguing that some form of Irish debt default is inevitable has been growing by the day. Whether making a moral case (Irish tax-payers should not be responsible for the debts of private banks) or a practical one (Irish tax-payers will prove unable to shoulder the likely debt burden now faced), such commentary has lead to an increasingly settled consensus in recent weeks. This consensus view is often adorned by the alleged comfort offered by the post-default experiences of Argentina, Russia or Kazakhstan and is expressed in a tone of growing impatience with the continuing failure of the Irish authorities to bow to the inevitable. I disagree.

The global financial crisis has impacted across different economies with varying degrees of severity. While countries such as China, Canada and Australia have been relatively unscathed, the previously booming Baltic region has been especially hard-hit. Latvian GDP, for example, contracted by almost 25% in 2008-2009, the unemployment rate rose from under 5% to over 17% and the government budget deficit for 2009 (under unchanged policies) was sent ballooning towards 18% of GDP.

Heightened doubts about the sustainability of the currency peg to the Euro in the face of the global crisis sparked a collapse in investor confidence, a flight of capital, a sudden contraction in credit and a sharp rise in the cost of government and bank borrowing. In effect, Latvia was engulfed by a cycle of vicious negativity that sent its economy into free fall.

The overwhelming consensus by the spring of 2009 was that devaluation and debt default was inevitable. Unable to access the debt markets, the Latvian authorities were forced to seek the external support of the IMF, the EU and their near Nordic neighbours and a package of loans was approved by the ECOFIN council in January 2009. Facing a continuing cycle of negativity, the inevitable devaluation and debt default was expected to follow and the yield (interest rate) on the Latvian (Euro-denominated) government bond maturing in March 2018 soared to almost 12% by March 2009.

With the continuing support of the international community, however, the Latvian authorities have implemented a range of policies that have restored the government finances to a credibly sustainable path. The consensus narrative of devaluation and default has come unstuck. There has been no break in the currency peg to the Euro. There has been no debt default. Fuelled by restored competitiveness, Latvian exports are booming and the economy is growing again. Confidence and capital have returned and the yield (interest rate) on the March 2018 government bond is now touching 5%. The inevitable of 18 months ago has turned out to be avoidable.

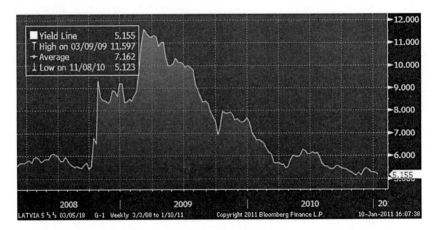

Some of the key policies implemented were:

- A 20% cut in the average public sector salary in the 2009 budget, followed by a further 5% reduction in the 2010 budget;
- A reduction in the number of government agencies from 76 to 39;
- A reduction in the number of hospitals from 59 to 42;
- An increase in the main VAT rate from 18% to 21%.

These and other measures have combined to put the Latvian government budget deficit on a sustainable path of below 10% of GDP in 2009, below 8.5% of GDP in 2010, below 6% of GDP in 2011 and below 3% of GDP in 2012.

Despite the extraordinary difficulties of recent years, Latvia has chosen to make the decisions to underpin its long-standing policy of becoming a credible member of the Euro-zone in 2014. The short-term attractions of a populist refusal to restore its government finances to a credibly sustainable path have been eschewed in favour of the long-term benefits of participating fully in the evolving European project.

The message for Ireland is clear. Debt default need not be the inevitable outcome of being engulfed in a cycle of vicious negativity and economic free fall. Economic recovery can be embarked upon without taking an existential risk with our banking system and currency. Our policy-makers are not powerless in battling a widely-expected inevitable slide into an experimental unknown.

By pursuing policies that return our government finances to a credibly sustainable path, the Irish authorities can follow the example of our Latvian neighbours and change the narrative of inevitable debt default into one of restored credibility and renewed prosperity. It need not be the case that we are locked into a static, vicious cycle of fiscal austerity, begetting low growth, begetting an intractable deficit and yet more austerity, which can only be broken by a dramatic default. A dynamic, virtuous alternative of fiscal credibility combined with regained cost competitiveness, begetting rising exports/revenue/confidence, begetting recovering growth and a narrowing deficit can be the path that Ireland follows. Indeed, the consistently improving trend in exports, output and exchequer returns over recent months, culminating in the better than forecast out-turn for 2010, suggests that this process possibly may be already underway. Despite the turmoil of recent times, the choice remains ours to make this a compelling certainty. There is nothing inevitable about our current predicament. We should look to Latvia.

7: LET'S NOT RISK SHATTERING THE MAGNIFICENT ILLUSION THAT IS THE MODERN BANKING SYSTEM

The Sunday Tribune, 16 January 2011

The modern banking system – the essential enabler of saving, investment, payment and exchange that provides the crucial 'blood-flow' of credit through the body of the modern economy – is a magnificent illusion.

Politicians, commentators and others who debate banking and slip comfortably into pronouncements about 'moral hazard' or 'burning bondholders' rarely seem to consider its frightening fragility or its illusory nature. While there may be some vague sense that modern banking involves a little more than the smooth recycling of savings into loans, there seems to be little consideration of how, at heart, it's a system of largely unthinking trust in a magnificent illusion.

Loans are just promises with greater or lesser likelihoods of being honoured. Deposits are mostly just claims on those promises. In effect, a stock of promises to repay has been made to banks by borrowers; banks, in turn, have used those promises (assets) to secure a stock of claims (liabilities) held by depositors/bondholders.

Into this trust-dependent system is then added the Janus-faced approach of promising depositors access to their 'money' on demand, having loaned most of this 'money' to business-owners or house-buyers from whom repayment will not be sought for many years into the future. To get a better sense of how these two potentially contradictory, but generally sustainable, commitments are being made by the modern bank, imagine borrowing money that you have committed to repay to a depositor on demand and, at the same time, loaning most of it to someone from whom you will not seek or receive repayment for the next 20 years or longer. This is the tightrope being walked hourly by the modern banking system.

Finally, ponder the key implication of this overall system: only a fraction of depositors' 'money' actually can be made available on demand – the rest is merely a claim on a promise. The successful blurring of this reality with the simultaneous provision of long-term credit is arguably the key underpinning of the modern economy and clearly depends on the trust of those who hold the claims to the promises – the depositors/bondholders. Lose that trust and the system unravels. Keep it and the system can flourish.

Fundamentally, this illusion has enabled the development of our modern, urban world of generally-rising prosperity, which, if shattered, would risk a chaotic return to a more brutish past:

- How much food and fuel does the typical urban-dweller store?

- How much economic activity and trade would survive a breakdown in exchange?

- How would countries that import essential food and energy secure supplies?

- How would society function to support the weak amid such potential breakdown?

These are just some of the questions that arise from any consideration of the consequences of the collapse of a modern banking system. The stakes are high, much higher than seems generally appreciated.

In the midst of continued deposit-flight and intensifying debate about how the liabilities of the Irish banking system can be lessened somewhat from the taxpayer's shoulders, let's reflect a little on the situation here.

Piecing together the latest published accounts, Central Bank releases and some reasonable approximations from informed anecdotal evidence, the current picture of the outstanding claims on our domestic banking institutions is likely close to this:

Domestic Irish Bank Liabilities	€ billion
Deposits	297
ECB and Irish CB	130
Senior Debt	72
Subordinate Debt	13
Total	**512**

It should be clear from the foregoing description of how the magnificent illusion of the banking system operates that maintaining the trust of these claimants should be the primary goal of all sensible policy. Becoming increasingly squeezed between 'the rock' of deposit-flight and 'the hard place' of greater reliance on the ECB is the place from which sensible policy should now be seeking to escape. In the same vein, any moral refreshment from burning some of the claims of the senior bondholders, for example, might prove very short-lived, if their fellow depositor claimants are prompted to accelerate their rush for the door.

Policy-making with a grasp of the relevant history seldom has seemed as important.

Though the antecedents of this illusionary system and its generally-beneficial effects can be traced to the goldsmiths of medieval Europe, the true conjuror of modern banking was probably US President, Franklin Delano Roosevelt. From the chaos of collapsing credit and economic stagnation, his pledge of the full authority of the United States government effectively restored trust to a banking and economic system paralysed by fear. Deposits, now insured by the federal government, returned to underpin the banking system and, through the workings of the magnificent illusion of modern banking, helped propel the US (and global) economy down a multi-decade path of expansion.

Do we really want to risk sundering this magnificent illusion for ourselves and others?

8: TIME TO FIND AN ANSWER TO IRELAND'S FUNDING FIX

The Sunday Business Post, 20 February 2011

The key challenge facing Ireland is to regain our economic sovereignty as soon as possible. In practice, this means successfully exiting our current dependence on the EU/IMF external facility by making a credible return to the debt markets. While recent months have seen much heat and, hopefully, a little light shed on the bigger question of how our deficit and banking challenges might be tackled to this end over the next few years, I want to focus solely on how we might bring some imagination to better meet some of our current funding needs over the more immediate term. In facing this battle, the sooner we can demonstrate an ability to source some funds from outside the external facility at an acceptable cost the better.

The fundamental reason for our current inability to access debt markets and our consequent dependence on the EU/IMF facility is that lenders lack confidence in our ability/willingness to repay our debts. In the words of Lorenzo Bini Smaghi of the ECB in a recent presentation on 'Sovereign Risk and the Euro':

> "The solvency of a sovereign is different from that of a company or a financial institution. Solvency of a sovereign depends on the ability/willingness … to: tax, cut expenditure and sell assets".

Simply put, those from whom we would like to borrow do not believe that we have the ability/willingness to raise the tax, cut the expenditure or sell the assets to repay that borrowing. While this may or may not prove to be the case, and it may well emerge in time that our political commitment and/or economic capacity to meet our obligations is being mistakenly underestimated, it seems likely that legitimate doubts on this score will remain for a prolonged period.

It need not follow, however, that we are powerless in attracting the attention of potential lenders and must remain passively resigned to complete dependence on the external facility for the foreseeable future. I believe that, with a little imagination, we can source some of the financing we currently need at an acceptable cost outside of the EU/IMF facility.

The key to this modest proposal is that, instead of our government offering the security of its currently mistrusted word to tax, cut and sell in sufficient size to make good on its debts, they offer something much more tangible: specifically designated assets and/or cash-flows. By providing potential lenders with absolute legal recourse to designated, ring-fenced security on which those lenders can put a credible value, the lenders will be in a position to lend against this security at a cost that is independent of our overall sovereign credit position – at a cost reflective of the credit-worthiness of the underlying asset and/or cash-flow security, and therefore likely to be lower than currently on offer from the EU/IMF. The much maligned credit rating agencies may well prove a positive influence in this regard.

While it is not my purpose to offer an exhaustive list of such assets and cash-flows, a couple of examples may be helpful in highlighting the general principle:

- The Review Group on State Assets and Liabilities, chaired by Colm McCarthy, is due to report within a matter of weeks to the incoming government. While I have no idea about its likely content, it seems more than reasonable to assume that it will list a substantial number of state assets that are currently unencumbered by any specifically designated liability. These assets are potentially available to provide the necessary security to currently untrusting lenders;

- There has been much debate and now general agreement that some form of both water metering and residential property tax are likely to be introduced as soon as practicable. An identifiable cash-flow consequently will accrue to the State from both these sources. In like fashion to the assets to be listed by McCarthy, these cash-flows also are potentially available to provide the necessary security to currently untrusting lenders.

The savings of Irish households has surged in recent years. The latest figures, released by the Central Statistics Office in October last, show the savings rate rising to over 12% in 2009 from a little over 4% the previous year to produce a net savings figure of over €11 billion for the year. There is every reason to believe that this trend intensified last year. In addition, therefore, to the usual domestic and international lenders who fund the State, a substantial pool of domestic savings is available to be attracted into a sufficiently secure and attractive vehicle.

We are currently scheduled to draw down €42.9 billion from the EU/IMF facility for 2010/2011 and a further €19.7 billion in 2012. Could not some proportion of this be raised alternatively (and more cheaply) *via* an asset/cash-flow secured savings vehicle designed with a little imagination?

9: ANY THREAT TO THE DOLLAR'S STATUS COULD HARM US INVESTMENTS

The Sunday Times, 27 March 2011

When Bobby Moore lifted the Jules Rimet trophy at Wembley in 1966, each pound sterling that he and his compatriots spent in celebration in the hostelries of London that summer evening would have bought them more than 11 deutschmarks. The crestfallen German players and supporters might have taken some comfort from their bitter defeat that day had they been able to foresee their subsequent World Cup victories in 1974 and 1990, and that each pound sterling in Bobby's pocket would barely buy the euro-equivalent of 2.25 of their beloved deutschmarks today. In a little over half an average lifetime, the pound sterling has lost over 80% of its purchasing power relative to its German counterpart.

The simple message for the investor is that when assessing how to maintain or increase your purchasing power through time, devoting some thought to how the custodians of any currency (government and/or central bank) to which you may be exposed are likely to treat that custodial duty may prove crucial. Relying on Her Majesty's Government and the Bank of England to maintain the relative purchasing power of sterling since that day of days for English football in 1966, for example, has proven to be a very expensive mistake.

In the face of a consistent tendency to consume more than it produces, the UK's policy-makers have consistently chosen to allow the purchasing power of the currency to diminish, rather than tackle fundamentally the over-consumption/under-production at the heart of the country's relative economic decline. Notwithstanding some brief periods of temporary upswing, such as when North-Sea oil revenues began to flow in the 1980s, sterling has proven to be over-valued at every exchange rate relative to the deutschmark since well before Alf Ramsey decided to play without wingers. There is nothing in the more recent policy choices of the UK authorities, and most especially in their response to the global financial crisis since 2007, to suggest any change in this long-standing trend. Enjoy a day trip to Newry and its environs with euros in your pocket to confirm the practical effect.

Given its greater relative significance in the world economy and investor portfolios, the key question I want to focus on is whether something similar could lie in store for the inheritors of the Anglo-Saxon crown across the Atlantic. Simply put, should the long-term investor now be shunning the US dollar?

Like the UK, the US economy is a persistent buyer of goods and services from the rest of the world in excess of the goods and services that it sells to the rest of the world. Everything else being equal, this would result in a greater supply of US dollars than demand for US dollars in the global foreign exchange market and a persistent loss of purchasing power *via* a persistent decline in the relative value of the dollar.

Fortunately for Uncle Sam, there are currently a number of countervailing buyers of dollars who combine to generally dilute, neutralise or reverse this supply/demand imbalance, ensuring that the value of the dollar is maintained at a level well in excess of what its persistent balance of payments deficit on current account would produce.

These include at least the following:

- Every central bank in the world has been a net buyer and consequent holder of the US dollar (and US dollar assets) in its role as the primary reserve currency of the global financial system. Ease of trade currently is ensured for these countries by possession of this globally-accepted 'store of value';

- Many countries that are in a persistent current account surplus position with the US also peg their exchange rate to the US dollar, necessitating their net buying and holding of the US dollar. The most conspicuous example in this respect is China, where the Bank of China has been a consistent net buyer and is now a holder of almost $2.85 trillion – a figure that has risen nearly six-fold in less than seven years (see chart below);

Foreign Exchange Reserves: China

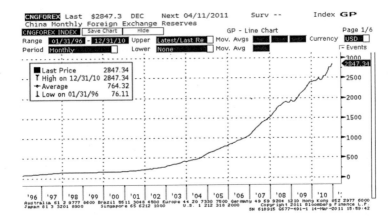

- Many commodities, most importantly oil, are priced in US dollars. If Sweden, for example, wants to buy oil from its Nordic neighbour Norway, it must buy US dollars to execute the transaction.

In summary, the position of the US dollar as the dominating reserve currency of the global financial system is the fundamental enabler of the US economy, over the last three decades, to persistently consume more than it produces without a major collapse in its purchasing power. Facing the harsh consequences of its payments imbalance so far has been avoidable. In like fashion to its reserve currency predecessor in the UK – which effectively lost this status with the sterling devaluation of 1967 – any diminution of this status for the dollar would see it exposed to the full reality of its fundamental over-supply.

While it is impossible to predict when, or even if, this will occur, it seems prudent to expect such a development would be met with the same policy disregard for the maintenance of purchasing power at the Federal Reserve on Constitution Avenue, Washington, as has proven to be the case at the Bank of England on Threadneedle Street, London. The long-term investor should doubt the commitment of the wielders of policy in the US to caring any more about fundamentally addressing their payments imbalance in the years ahead than their counterparts in the UK have shown since a certain Russian linesman broke German hearts nearly 45 years ago.

It might be time to check your exposure to the greenback.

10: IGNORE THE PROPHETS OF FISCAL DOOM AND GO FOR THE DOUBLE

The Sunday Times, 10 April 2011

A strong prospect of doubling your money in a little over seven years is a rare investment opportunity – and one that is now available on our doorstep. Because of the current fear about our debts, Irish sovereign 10-year bonds offer an annual return hovering around 10%. I believe there is a strong likelihood that this is a mispricing of historic proportion.

Financial markets operate in a permanent fog of uncertainty. They are prone to reach for the often faulty lamp of a flawed, simple story to help illuminate their way along a usually precarious path. Following the introduction of the Euro, for example, the simple story of a single currency equating to a broadly single interest rate/credit risk prompted an enormous flow of core country savings to eager peripheral borrowers. Overlooked by a regulatory regime seemingly asleep to the requirements of a radically-changed environment, banks competed feverishly to promote, facilitate and profit from this frenzied flow. We are still grappling with the consequences.

In a similar vein, financial markets now risk embracing a flawed, simple story in relation to the likely path of the Irish economy. As commonly recited by those in the big-tent of Nobel-winning and other widely-lauded economists, the usual Euro-sceptic UK voices and a range of Irish commentators across the political divide, a simple story of fiscal austerity, begetting lower growth, begetting more austerity and a further choking of growth, in a vicious cycle that can only be broken by an inevitable debt default, has become the settled narrative.

A 10-year sovereign bond yield touching 10% is an obvious confirmation of this conviction. The more complex possibility of a dynamic, virtuous cycle is being largely ignored.

Since the Whitaker/Lemass reforms of the late 1950s, the Irish economy has performed spectacularly. The transition from being a basic producer of bulk agricultural product, dependent on the often-volatile UK market, to being a broadly-based largely services-providing economy exporting across the globe has been a dramatically positive one.

The economy has expanded by over 4% a year on average since 1960, bringing the income per person in Ireland from below 2/3rds of our EU peers then, to almost 1.25 times that peer group today.

While many factors, both domestic and international, have contributed to this outcome, the emergence of Ireland as a major hub for US corporate investment undoubtedly has played a key role. The Irish share of US corporate investment in the EU is currently 8%, which is actually more than total US investment in the so-called BRIC (Brazil, Russia, India and China) economies. The announcement in recent weeks of the increasing investment of Intel in Ireland is just one example suggesting a continued significant flow from this source.

A further contributing factor has been the particularly favourable demographic profile of the Irish population. With the birth rate peaking as recently as 1980, compared to up to 35 years earlier for most of our peers, the flow of young and increasingly educated participants into our labour force continues to give a strong underpinning to both potential output and domestic demand. Though constrained for many well-worn reasons over the last two and a half years, the sharply rising savings rate over this period can be viewed as reflecting the deferred potential of this underlying demand. This is a pent-up potential that may be sparked by little more than the passage of time. After all, many purchases cannot be postponed indefinitely.

The combination of fiscal profligacy and international recession saw Ireland's public finances become increasingly strained in the early to mid-1980s. The budget deficit as a percentage of GDP climbed into double-digits for a number of years and the government debt to GDP ratio shot up to over 106% of GDP by 1987. The consensus expectation that the inevitable fiscal adjustment would choke growth for many years *via* the familiar vicious cycle was widely held. A period of prolonged stagnation, leading to a probable collapse of the punt and/or a default on government debt, was widely anticipated. A 10-year sovereign bond yield over 11% in late 1986 confirmed this consensus.

In the event, the combination of the confidence generated by determined fiscal action and the increasingly favourable external environment sparked a dynamic, virtuous cycle of fiscal credibility, begetting rising consumer confidence/falling funding costs, begetting a recovery in growth, begetting a narrower deficit/greater fiscal credibility and so on. Many who conflated Irish growth potential with that of our less flexible, more closed economy neighbours were seriously mistaken. The inevitable of early 1987 turned out to be the avoidable, as the Irish economy set down a dynamic path of robust, unbroken growth for the next 20 years.

Ireland has long been a dynamic, open economy with a history of achieving strong growth. The continuing potential for further expansion is underpinned, at least, by a particularly supportive environment for the continuing attraction of US (and other) corporate investment and by an unusually supportive demographic profile. In addition, our experience of coming through the comparable challenges of the 1980s underlines our capacity to avoid recourse to the potential pariah status of default, and should strengthen our belief that the static, vicious cycle predicted so widely at the moment will be trumped by a dynamic, virtuous cycle in the years ahead.

Indeed, the consistently improving trend in exports, output and exchequer returns over recent months, culminating in the better than forecast out-turn for 2010, suggests that this process may possibly be already underway. Another example of financial markets being misled by the surface plausibility of a flawed, simple story could well be in the offing. Irish sovereign bond yields at current levels may well be remembered as a mispricing of historic dimension.

11: SIDESTEP HOPE AND GET TURNED ON BY UTILITIES

The Sunday Times, 8 May 2011

Every stock investor is faced with the greater or lesser risk that the economics of the business that they have invested in (or may invest in) may come undone at any time. To a greater or lesser extent we are all engaged in the process of what James Montier of GMO calls 'capitalising hope'.

It is no surprise, therefore, that to lessen this dependence on 'hope', many investors spend huge effort trying to identify companies that may possess some protective moat – an endeavour whose motivation and difficulty was neatly summarised in a recent comment piece: 'Buffett-ites or Bluff-it-ites' from the Value Investment Institute:

> "It's important to remember that companies with real sustainable moats are not the norm. Collectively, humans are creative and greedy and, where possible, others will try to muscle in on attractive opportunities. Inevitably, some high return businesses will be made ordinary. Corporate history is littered with moats-that-weren't ... The consequences of a misdiagnosis can be severe".

A great brand can fall out of favour, a successful patent can expire without replacement, a remarkable technology can be bettered, an entrenched oligopolistic structure can be dislodged; these are just some of the risks faced by the stock investor in a wide range of companies, where the protective moat may be breached with likely disastrous consequences for returns.

Against this backdrop, the significant exposure of Warren Buffett, the most successful and passionate proponent of investing with the benefit of a 'protective moat', to regulated utilities is an obvious source of interest. The rationale of the Sage of Omaha for such an exposure to this sector, second only in size to his legendary investment in insurance, certainly seems worth trying to understand.

This summary explanation from his 2009 letter to shareholders in Berkshire Hathaway is better than any possible words of mine:

> "Our regulated electric utilities, offering monopoly service in most cases, operate in a symbiotic manner with the customers in their service areas, with those users depending on us to provide first-class service and invest for their future needs. Permitting and construction periods for generation and major transmission facilities stretch way out, so it is incumbent on us to be far-sighted. We, in turn, look to our utilities' regulators (acting on behalf of our customers) to allow us an appropriate return on the huge amounts of capital we must deploy to meet future needs. We shouldn't expect our regulators to live up to their end of the bargain unless we live up to ours.
>
> MidAmerican has consistently kept its end of the bargain with society and, to society's credit, it has reciprocated: With few exceptions, our regulators have promptly allowed us to earn a fair return on the ever-increasing sums of capital we must invest. Going forward ... We believe that ... we will be allowed the return we deserve on the funds we invest".

For Buffett, the risk of a moat-breach for the investor in regulated utilities is materially less than is the case in so many other areas of potential investment. Crucially, however, this lessening of dependence on 'hope' is on offer without compromising the likelihood of earning 'the return we deserve on the funds we invest'. It is this combination that he views as compelling and underpins the rationale for his large exposure to this sector.

In order to illustrate this in practice, I'm going to concentrate on a UK example, United Utilities (UU), at the time of its last regulatory review in November 2009, though in principle the arguments are applicable more generally. Although we bought UU for a number of our globally-diversified funds in early 2009, it is important to emphasise that this example is chosen purely for illustrative reasons and is in no way a recommendation.

UU is the appointed water and wastewater service provider in the North West of England, serving around seven million people. Like all regulated utilities, UU is permitted to achieve a regulated return on its regulated capital value (RCV). The return permitted is determined by the regulator, OFWAT, on a five-year cycle. The latest determination was in November 2009 for the 2010 to 2015 period.

The key metric from a shareholder perspective determined by OFWAT is the calculation of the expected, real cost of equity to UU over the next five-year cycle. This, in turn, becomes the expected real return on equity that OFWAT 'allows' UU to make over this period.

OFWAT calculates this metric using a methodology based on the capital asset pricing model (CAPM) and the figure for UU (for the period 2010 to 2015) was 7.1% (note: in arriving at this calculation, OFWAT also assumes a capital structure of 58% debt/42% equity – any greater gearing than this would increase the return to the shareholder and *vice versa*).

For ease of illustration, I'm going to assume that UU was priced at one times RCV (note: at the time of the regulatory determination in November 2009, it was on offer in the market at around 0.9 times RCV) and also assume that UU has the capital structure assumed by OFWAT. On this basis, the allowed real return on offer to a shareholder in UU was 7.1% – a level that I believe comfortably met the criterion of being 'the return we deserve on the funds we invest' for the shareholder/potential shareholder.

Another useful framework for considering the Buffett rationale may be through the following definitions:

- **Equity Risk Premium** is the excess return that an individual stock or the overall stock market provides over a risk-free rate. This excess return compensates investors for taking on the relatively higher risk of the equity market;

- *Ex ante* is Latin for 'beforehand'. In models where there is uncertainty that is resolved during the course of events, the *ex ante* values (for example, of expected gain) are those that are calculated in advance of the resolution of uncertainty;

- **Ex post** is Latin for 'after the fact'. In models where there is uncertainty that is resolved during the course of events, the *ex post* values (for example, of expected gain) are those that are calculated after the uncertainty has been resolved.

In summary and using this framework, Buffett sees regulated utilities as offering the stock investor the strong likelihood of being an *ex post* capturer of the 'equity risk premium' in an otherwise more uncertain *ex ante* world for alternative uses of his money. The ongoing enormous exposure that he maintains to the regulated utility sector is therefore understandable, as he does his best to side-step 'hope' without sacrificing return: the endeavour that investors everywhere should be seeking to emulate.

12: DON'T BELIEVE THE HYPE, DO YOUR OWN RESEARCH

The Sunday Times, 12 June 2011

The success of value investing over many decades understandably has produced a large body of speculation grappling to explain this outcome. Many are now looking for answers in the growing study of behavioural finance. In the following discussion, I want to touch on the possibility of one particular behavioural bias potentially playing a role.

The greater part of human history has seen mass acceptance of the certainties conveyed by a voice of apparent authority. The pronouncements of Pope, Patriarch or descendent of the Prophet have been adhered to by largely unquestioning multitudes content to assume the accuracy of a superior, external wisdom. The fact that we now know, for example, that the earth isn't flat and that it orbits the sun as opposed to the other way around has done little to dim this adherence. Similarly, the competing isms that have jockeyed and clashed in more recent centuries have attracted followers who generally have offered undoubting belief regardless of any contrary evidence.

It seems that part of our successful struggle for survival down the harsh millennia is an evolved instinct to settle on an apparently authoritative source to frame our decision-making. We seem to be hardwired to need this external reference point to do much of our thinking for us as we navigate gingerly through the uncertainties of life. It may well have been what kept our ancestors alive in the unforgiving physical struggle that has characterised most of human experience since Adam developed a taste for fruit.

This instinct to accept the short-cut provided by accepting an external reference point also is apparent in our investment decision-making. In this case, the external reference point is provided by the all-knowing 'market', where the unquestioning adherents of 'efficient markets' chant their unshakeable belief that the price of any asset reflects all known information and therefore must be 'rational' and unquestioned. Like their religious and other antecedents, many academics, investors and policy-makers are now susceptible to delegating much of their thinking to the almighty authority of the 'market'. This devotion was probably best displayed by an allegedly agitated Eugene Fama, the acknowledged 'father' of the efficient markets hypothesis, when he loudly informed a doubter of market efficiency at a conference some years ago that:

"God knows that markets are efficient!".

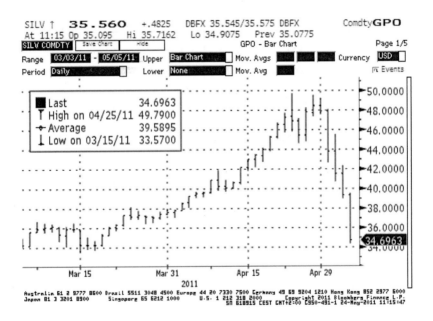

The spot price of silver closed at $48.44 an ounce on Thursday, 28 April 2011, and fell almost 30% by the following Thursday, 5 May – see the graph above. An exhaustive search for 'news' to explain this rapid price change yields little. It seems just one more on the long list of examples of the inconvenient truth that, far from being 'rational', the much relied upon 'market' is often a hugely misleading basis on which to frame a decision. The importance of this relates to all markets at all times and is by no means confined to commodities such as silver. This is the territory in which the disciplined, thinking value investor seems primed to flourish.

A brief consideration of just some of the factors impacting 'price' across a number of asset classes helps highlight why:

- **Stocks:** The growing number of passive investors buying and selling stocks purely to replicate an arbitrary index and thereby impacting on price in a way that has nothing to do with value;

- **Bonds:** The largest holder of the market against which all are benchmarked, the US Treasury market, is the US Central Bank with nearly 9%, closely followed by China with around 8%, both impacting global bond prices and interest rates in a way that has nothing to do with value;

- **Commodities:** It is arguable that, in the absence of an income stream, the price of commodities is by definition nothing more than a speculative stab at what the next trader will pay – once again having little or nothing to do with value.

A closely-related phenomenon to our instinct to follow the apparent certainties of an external authority is our strong tendency to take unthinking comfort in some conventional wisdom. Just as an unquestioned belief in the authority of something like the 'market' can prove damaging to our bank balance, so too can lazy acceptance of the apparently obvious as often offered by some convincingly-argued conventional wisdom.

A favourite example of the perils of conventional wisdom is from the always interesting *Economist* in 1985. In a piece to mark the 40th anniversary of the Cold War division of Europe, and undoubtedly reflecting the conventional wisdom of the time, the authoritative analysis concluded that the prospects for a change in the *status quo* in Europe were all but non-existent and that "nothing much will have changed by 2025". We now know that, within six weeks of the publication of this piece, the transformation of Europe had begun as Gorbachev met Reagan in Reykjavik.

The key lesson for the investor is that we seem to have a greater likelihood of succeeding by constantly battling our inherited instinct to accept without question the apparent wisdom of an external authority like the 'market'. In addition, we must be constantly wary of falling for an unthinking acceptance of all prevailing conventional wisdom. A disciplined refusal to make an investment decision based on the guidance offered by any 'market', or on some soothing story that chimes with the general view, seems likely to enhance our chance of success, and may be playing some role in the continued success of value investors. We could do worse than keeping the words of the great US value investor Joel Greenblatt uppermost in our thinking:

> "Don't trust anyone over 30. And don't trust anyone 30 and under. Do your own work".

13: ENDA, TIME TO PUT SOME SKIN IN THE GAME

Business and Finance, July 2011

It has been a remarkable year and a half for the Taoiseach. He prevailed in the challenge to his party leadership. He led his party to an historic election victory. Over six months in power, he still basks in the popularity of a prolonged political 'honeymoon'.

However, there is no denying the unnerving truth that continues to stare us all in the face: the word of Enda Kenny is generally disbelieved. So, too, is that of Michael Noonan, Patrick Honohan and all of those in charge of our public finances who say that Ireland's sovereign debt will be repaid. This is not my opinion (I'm actually part of the minority who believe them), but it is the undeniable, collective opinion of savers across the Euro-zone. The word of the Taoiseach is so mistrusted among his own citizens and those of our Euro-zone partners that they are demanding almost 8% *per annum* to loan money to his government for the next 10 years. Clearly, the collective opinion is that our Taoiseach is being economical with the truth or deluded when he tells the world: "We will repay our loans; we will not restructure our debt".

As we saw in 2008, and on numerous other occasions here and elsewhere in the past, when trust in the head of government collapses, public discourse disintegrates towards farce and worse. That may be amusing for a time when people feel generally secure and can enjoy a little banter about money being won 'on the horses', but in the current environment of great fear about the future, such generalised dismissal of the word of the Taoiseach holds great potential danger.

As a matter of urgency, the Taoiseach needs to gain trust. Let there be no doubt, this is a task well within the remit of the powers at his disposal. It is not dependent on the decisions of others in Athens, Berlin or elsewhere, or on how our economy may or may not progress in the period ahead. As Taoiseach with a commanding majority, and in stark contrast to his beleaguered counterpart in the White House for example, Enda Kenny has all the decision-making freedom necessary. It is solely a question of whether he has the will to make the decisions needed to gain the trust of a currently unbelieving world.

Unfortunately, the shadow of handsomely-pensioned ex-Ministers, civil servants and Taoisigh whose credibility lie in tatters but have suffered no personal loss is a long one. To begin to build trust, the Taoiseach needs to offer something beyond the ordinary. He needs to outline a non-standard commitment with which to convince the doubters that Ireland will honour its sovereign debts.

My suggestion for this is a simple one. Just as his predecessor had the conviction to chart a new path with a 'Constitutional Crusade' 30 years ago, the Taoiseach should now lead a crusade for our country to regain its economic sovereignty. In the run-up to the crucial December budget, and building on the positive momentum of the better programme and economic news of recent months, he should announce a 'Sovereignty Crusade'.

The centrepiece of this 'Sovereignty Crusade' should be a solemn covenant between the Taoiseach and the Irish people:

> The terms of the current programme of deficit reduction, which will see the current budget deficit at 3% of GDP in 2015, will be met. Failure to achieve this target will see Taoiseach and Cabinet Ministers retire from public life with no pension.

> In addition, the Taoiseach and his Cabinet colleagues have agreed to have their personal net worth independently audited and to invest half of this in the Irish 10-year sovereign bond.

I believe that such commitments would immediately confer trust on our Taoiseach and his Cabinet colleagues and remove many of the doubts about Ireland honouring our sovereign debts.

Indeed, this is a commitment that the Taoiseach should suggest also to his counterparts in Portugal, Spain and Italy at the summit gathering this weekend. The example of these governments, lead by Ireland, making such a major personal commitment to the 'no default' policies that they are all espousing could transform public and market perception for the good of all.

It's time to put some skin in the game, Taoiseach. Announce a 'Sovereignty Crusade', make your covenant with the Irish people, and reach for your place in history!

14: WHEN ECONOMIC BOOM TURNS TO BUST, BLAME IT ON NIXON

The Sunday Times, 7 July 2011

There has been much discussion about the recent travails of the Irish economy: how could 'boom' turn to 'bust' so dramatically? To help understand one aspect of what has happened and why, I think we need to pay a brief visit back to the White House and the controversial rule of 'Tricky Dick'. Of little focus in this context to date, I believe the events on Pennsylvania Avenue a generation ago are crucial to understanding what has befallen the Irish economy.

Richard Nixon is generally remembered as the disgraced President at the heart of the Watergate cover-up. Others remember his dogged continuation of the doomed escapade in Vietnam, or more generously, his opening of relations with Communist China. By comparison, there is little discussion of the decision he took on the night of 15 August 1971, which has arguably done more to shape our world than any single decision taken by anyone: his stunning and unexpected order to 'shut the gold window'.

The monetary structure of the post-war world was constructed at the famous Bretton Woods conference in July 1944. The soon-to-be victorious allies, with the United States now the dominant leader, were determined to build a credible and durable monetary structure to promote trade and recovery. The cornerstone of this structure was that the 44 countries at the meeting agreed to peg their currencies to the US dollar, which in turn was pegged to gold at a rate of $35 per ounce; in effect, the monetary structure of the world was now anchored to the dollar, which in turn was anchored to gold. Against this backdrop of monetary stability, post-war global trade expanded enormously, helping to fuel a rapid and sustained global recovery. The hopes of the architects at Bretton Woods were more than fulfilled as the benefits of a stable monetary structure, anchored *via* the dollar on gold, seemed to be broadly accepted and understood.

The chink in this structure proved to be the implicit necessity for the anchor country, the United States, to manage its economy so that its peg to gold remained credible. Those who held dollars needed to believe that their dollars would always be convertible into gold: the anchor store of value.

In replicating his immediate predecessors by refusing to curtail a growing balance of payments deficit, resulting in a quickening flow of dollars to the rest of the world, Nixon fatally undermined the credibility of dollar convertibility to gold. The persistent appearance of France, in particular, at the 'gold window', seeking to convert its growing stock of dollars into gold, left Nixon with an unenviable decision to make on that hot August night almost 40 years ago – continue to convert the dollars presented at the window into gold and thereby exhaust the gold reserves of the United States, or refuse to do so and smash the cornerstone of the global monetary structure. He chose the latter and the current global monetary system was born.

In words applicable to all modern central banks, Nobel laureate Paul Krugman summarised the new order:

> "The current world monetary system assigns no special role to gold; indeed, the Federal Reserve is not obliged to tie the dollar to anything. It can print as much or as little money as it deems appropriate".

Although never inevitable, the extraordinary boom and bust of the Irish economy is a direct consequence of this system. Following the introduction of the Euro, Irish banks chose to transform themselves into giant vacuum cleaners, sucking in vast quantities of generally short-term savings from every nook and cranny of the Euro-zone, and disgorging the vast bulk of these savings on a long-term basis into the eager hands of Irish property players.

In our anchorless monetary system, subject only to banks continuing to meet some arbitrary capital ratios, this suction and disgorgement was able to grow to grotesque levels. The European Central Bank, narrowly focused on its Euro-zone inflation mandate and content to supply as much 'reserves' as demanded by the system at its target interest rate, mirrored the neutral bystander role of its sleeping agent in Dame Street. A near trebling in the outstanding stock of suction (borrowing) and disgorgement (lending) by Irish banks in the six years to 2008 was the stunning outcome (see the graph below from the *Nyberg Report*).

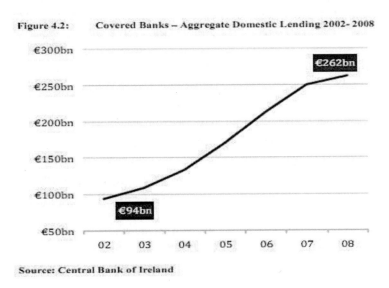

Figure 4.2:   **Covered Banks – Aggregate Domestic Lending 2002- 2008**

Source: Central Bank of Ireland

The words of the great J.K. Galbraith have never seemed as apt:

> "The process by which banks create money is so simple that it repels the mind".

Soaring property prices, construction and related employment, and government revenue and expenditure were accelerating features of the economy through this period. A boom of historic proportion then hit a shuddering halt, as the providers of short-term lending to the Irish banks have increasingly looked for their money back over the last three years.

The volatile legacy of Nixon: a global monetary system, in which the process of credit/debt creation by the banking system has no hard anchor, has proven to be brutally destructive for the Irish economy. In combination with the madness and myopia that infected Irish banking and political decision-making through the boom, the Nixon decision to 'shut the gold window' has left us in a hostile sea of debt, hoping to navigate a way back to the shore of economic sovereignty. It's proving to be a choppy ride.

15: FED'S RESPONSE MAY HIGHLIGHT ITS WEAKNESS

The Sunday Business Post, 7 August 2011

The Great Depression following the Wall Street crash of 1929 has been widely blamed on the flawed policy response of the US Federal Reserve. Most famously, the father of monetary economics, Milton Friedman, argued that the collapse of the US money supply by a third between 1929 and 1933 turned a brutal day on the stock market into a multi-year depression. In Friedman's view, the failure of the Federal Reserve to maintain the money supply caused the vicious cycle of collapsing banks, activity and hope:

> "The Federal Reserve System could have prevented the decline (in the money supply) at all times. The terrible depression which followed the crash was a direct result of bungling by the Federal Reserve System".

This view was powerfully endorsed by current Fed Chairman Ben Bernanke in his remarks at Friedman's 90th birthday celebration in 2002:

> "Let me end my talk by abusing slightly my status as an official representative of the Federal Reserve. I would like to say to Milton and Anna: Regarding the Great Depression. You're right, we did it. We're very sorry. But thanks to you, we won't do it again".

Central to the views of Friedman, Bernanke and many others is the assumed ability of the Federal Reserve to determine the money supply. In simple terms, as the controller of the dollar printing press, the Federal Reserve is assumed to control the quantity of money in the economy – known as the money supply. In practice, the mechanism by which the Fed is assumed to exercise this control is familiar to all who have had the dubious pleasure of sitting through an economics class on the 'money multiplier'.

Assume that the reserve ratio set by the Fed for the banking system is 10% and assume that the Fed wants to increase the money supply by $1,000. Effectively, it prints $100 of notes/'reserves' and uses them to buy $100 of US Treasury Bonds on the open market. The seller of the bonds deposits her $100 proceeds at her bank, which puts $10 aside as a reserve and loans out $90 to a customer looking to pay his gas bill. The gas company deposits its $90 proceeds at its bank, which puts $9 aside as a reserve and loans out $81 to a customer looking to go to the opera. The opera company deposits its $81 proceeds at its bank and the process continues until a total of $1,000 in 'new money' has been 'created' – the policy objective of the Fed to increase the money supply by $1,000 has been achieved.

Crucial to this story is not the oft-commented wonder of the multiplier, but the direction of causation – the Fed determines the money supply and we can all rest assured that, having learned the lessons of the 1930s, that it has the necessary wisdom and policy levers to avoid a repeat.

Unfortunately, there is an alternative view of how the money supply is determined, which is so at odds with that of Friedman and Bernanke that it brings to mind the story of Samuel Beckett when asked by a French journalist: *"Vous êtes Anglais, Monsieur Beckett?"*. To which Beckett replied: *'Au contraire'*. In fact, this alternative view of money supply determination runs in completely the reverse direction, and was summarised well by the Senior Vice President of the New York Fed, Alan Holmes, in 1969:

> "In the real world, banks extend credit, creating deposits in the process, and look for reserves later".

While this view has many implications, its relevance here is that the Fed does not determine the money supply. In practice, while the Fed certainly can print dollars/'reserves' and buy US Treasury bonds, it has no way of ensuring that this will cause lending/borrowing into the economy by the banking system and its customers respectively.

The collapse of Lehman Brothers in September 2008 froze the global credit system and threatened to plunge the global economy into a depression. As trust between banks, and between banks and their customers, was shaken violently, global trade and activity collapsed in a frightening downward spiral. Many feared that a depression of 1930s dimensions was underway.

The dramatic response of the Fed under Bernanke, no doubt driven by the lessons that he and Friedman had drawn from the Great Depression, has seen the Fed effectively print an unprecedented amount of dollars/'reserves' to buy an unprecedented amount of US Treasury (and other) Bonds. Under the strange moniker of 'quantitative easing', this response either has been widely praised for having averted a depression, or widely criticised for being an inevitable precursor to runaway inflation.

The alternative view, however, is that the Fed deserves neither praise nor criticism. Stemming from the views of Holmes and others, its powerlessness in determining the money supply has rendered it largely irrelevant. Even allowing for the fact that the Fed now pays interest on the 'excess reserves' of the banking system, their huge build-up at the Fed is one possible confirmation of this view.

As a heavily-indebted populace has shown little appetite to borrow, even at historically-low interest rates, and as the calls for 'QE3' grow louder in the wake of the Tea Party hobbling of the fiscal lever, the troubling question of whether Fed power is little more than a delusion looks likely to loom larger for investors everywhere.

16: WITHOUT TRUST, THE BANKS ARE STUCK

The Sunday Business Post, 4 September 2011

It is becoming clearer that the recurring financial turmoil since the collapse of Lehman Brothers almost three years ago is caused fundamentally by the risk of collapsing trust in the global banking system, and that this must dominate central bank thinking for the foreseeable future. This may best be understood by considering a simple example of how a modern bank creates money by granting a loan:

- A bank grants a loan of €10,000 to a customer to buy a car. The bank credits the current account of the customer, who writes a cheque for €10,000 to the seller of the car;

- The seller of the car deposits the cheque to her bank account. If this is the same bank as that of the car-buyer, this bank now has an 'asset' in the form of the loan to the car-buyer, funded by a 'liability' in the form of the deposit from the car-seller. Alternatively, if the car-seller deposits the cheque at a different bank, the bank of the car-buyer will borrow €10,000 *via* the inter-bank market to transfer to the bank of the car-seller, and while having the same 'asset' as before, it is now funded in the form of this inter-bank loan.

The net effect of this process is that €10,000 has been created from nothing and is now circulating in the economy. The bank that granted the loan profits from charging a higher interest rate to its car-buying customer than it pays to either the car-selling depositor or, in the alternative case, to the inter-bank lender. This profit potential incentivises the bank to repeat the process as often and to the largest extent possible.

The regulatory constraint on this is theoretically two-fold:

- The bank must fulfil a 'reserve ratio' – in other words, it must hold a certain percentage of its liabilities in 'reserve' at the central bank. While, in theory, this enables the central bank to control the quantum of loans granted by the bank, in practice the central bank must acquiesce to the lending decisions of the bank by ensuring that sufficient reserves are always available for the bank to meet its 'reserve ratio'. In effect, there is no 'reserve' constraint on the bank loaning and thereby creating as much money as it chooses. This reality was summarised well by economist Basil J. Moore in 1983:

  > "Once deposits have been created by an act of lending, the central bank must ensure that the required reserves are available. Otherwise the banks, no matter how hard they scramble for funds, could not in aggregate meet their reserve requirements".

- The bank must also fulfil a 'capital ratio' – in other words, it must hold a certain percentage of capital, such as equity provided by its shareholders, to its assets, such as loans. While again, in theory, this enables the central bank to control the quantum of loans granted by the bank, in practice, a bank determined to grant more loans is free both to increase its capital *via* retained profits and/or to raise fresh capital without any interference from the central bank. In effect, there is little 'capital' constraint on the bank loaning and thereby creating as much money as it chooses.

Now consider the impact of any doubt emerging about the ability or willingness of the car-buying borrower to repay his loan. Concerned about the security of their money, the car-selling depositor or the inter-bank lender is likely to seek immediate repayment from the car-buyer's bank. Unable to seek immediate repayment from the car-buying borrower, or to source funding elsewhere as doubt about its loan-book spreads, the bank is forced to source the funds it needs from the central bank.

This is the predicament of many banks across the Euro-zone periphery. Widely-voiced doubt about the ability or willingness of their borrowing customers (individuals or governments) to repay their loans has sparked a flight of deposits and a recalling of inter-bank loans, leaving these banks hugely reliant on funding provided by the ECB. In the case of our 'covered' banks, for example, this ECB and Irish central bank funding is now around €150 billion.

More recently, the possibility that doubt about Euro-zone banks may impact elsewhere has begun to emerge. Many of the larger Euro-zone banks, for example, have substantial operations in the United States, and rumours that they are having difficulty continuing to access the required dollar funding have grown louder. In particular, it has been widely reported that a major Euro-zone bank was unable to access a required $500m in funding in recent weeks and was forced to turn to the ECB. If true, this in turn would have forced the ECB to turn to the Fed to source the required dollars.

It is *via* such a process that the paralysing infection of doubt so apparent in many Euro-zone banks could mutate into a disease that attacks the global banking system. The likely consequences of this are unknowable, as the Nixon-ignited 'money-creation' engine of modern banking is potentially shunted into reverse to become a 'money-destroying' monster. This potential nightmare on main-street likely unites Bernanke, Trichet and King in sleeplessness. Low interest rates for a long time seem unavoidable.

17: BLOCK OUT THE NOISE AND SELECT INVESTMENTS WITH REAL MEANING

The Sunday Times, 11 September 2011

Dramatic footage of frenzied traders gesticulating wildly in front of flashing screens is the popular image of financial markets and those who operate in them. It seems that every twist and turn of the stock, bond or currency markets is now a staple segment of traditional television news broadcasts, not to mention the proliferation of channels that are now devoted to dissecting every blip across the financial market landscape. Unfortunately, most of the activity on show and the 'news' that drives it is worthless.

The reason why is clear when applied to some sporting examples:

- Imagine you had the opportunity of playing golf against Rory McElroy. Consider whether your chances of shooting a lower score than him are greater or lesser over one hole, one round, or one tournament?

- As a further embellishment of your sporting dreams, imagine you had the chance of playing tennis against Rafael Nadal. Consider whether your chances of winning are greater or lesser after a point, after a game, or after a set?

- As the Premier League circus gathers steam, consider whether the chances of Manchester United lying lower on the league table than say Wolves are greater or lesser after the first half-dozen matches, at Christmas, or at the end of the season?

The 'meaning' in these examples is that Rory McElroy is a better golfer than you, Rafael Nadal a better tennis player and that Manchester United, though it pains me to say it, is a better football team than

Wolves. Clearly, the longer the time-frame considered the greater the likelihood of 'meaning' and the lesser the likelihood of 'noise' in the outcome. This is as true for investors as it is for golfers, tennis players or football teams.

The trader and 'Philosopher of the Black Swan', Nassim Taleb, put it characteristically well in his classic book, *Fooled by Randomness: The Hidden Role of Chance in Life and in the Markets*:

> "Over a short time increment, one observes the variability of a portfolio, not the returns. When I see an investor monitoring his portfolio with live prices on his cellular telephone or his handheld, I smile and smile. The same methodology can explain why the news is full of noise and why it is better to read *The New Yorker* on Mondays than *The Wall Street Journal* every morning (from the standpoint of frequency, aside from the massive gap of intellectual class between the two publications)".

Stock-investors, however, have been rushing in the opposite direction. Bombarded by more and more 'news' from a rapidly expanding media, they have been shortening their time-frame and thereby tilting the basis for their decisions increasingly away from 'meaning' and towards 'noise'. A good proxy illustration of this is the average holding period for stocks.

Chart 9: NYSE average holding period, 1940-2005

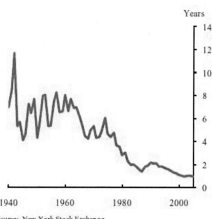

Source: New York Stock Exchange

The trend on the NYSE, where the average holding period for stocks is now just six months, compared to over six years in the late 1970s, is true of stock-markets everywhere (see chart above).

Taleb is also well-known for his clash with many of the followers of Warren Buffett. This quote, also from *Fooled by Randomness*, has provoked particular scorn:

> "I am not saying that Warren Buffett is not skilled; only that a large population of random investors will *almost necessarily* produce someone with his track record *just by luck*".

The irony of this is that Buffett takes the mirror opposite approach to investing than the legions of noise-driven, short-term traders who so obviously offend Taleb's insights and sensibility. Buffett is famously unconcerned by the vagaries of short-term 'news' and has held some of his favoured stock investments, such as Gillette and Coca-Cola, for decades. Together with his friend and business-partner Charlie Munger, his approach is the antithesis of the news-obsessed day-traders dismissed by Taleb as, at best, lucky fools:

> "We like to buy businesses. We don't like to sell and we expect the relationship to last a lifetime".

Implicitly accepting Taleb's logic, Buffett has translated his stock-picking prowess and the discipline to wait for 'meaning' to trump 'noise' into the greatest investment record in history. As they both strive to avoid the 'noise', it seems that the Sage of Omaha and the Philosopher of the Black Swan may have more in common than either might want to admit and that, as investors in a period of particular turbulence, we all could do worse than trying to follow their example.

18: EUROPEAN CENTRAL BANK MUST ACT TO REIN IN UNRULY HERD

The Sunday Times, 25 September 2011

Hungry fast-food customers in New York currently pay a little over $6 for a Big Mac meal. Their fellow burger-lovers in Dublin shell out the equivalent of around $9.50, while the same indulgence in Zurich now costs close to a whopping $17. While there may be some relative cost differences that explain some of the discrepancy in price across the three cities, and maybe even account fully for the difference between New York and Dublin, the relative price charged in Zurich has no economic rationale.

The well-documented herd behaviour of financial markets, which in the past has been manifest in everything from tulips to Irish bank stocks, is clearly rampant again. Feasting off the fear of nervous investors everywhere, a favoured 'risk-aversion' trade of the speculative herd over recent months has been to buy Swiss francs. The trade-weighted value of the affectionately-known 'Swissie' spiked over 27% between the middle of April and 10 August 2011 (see chart below).

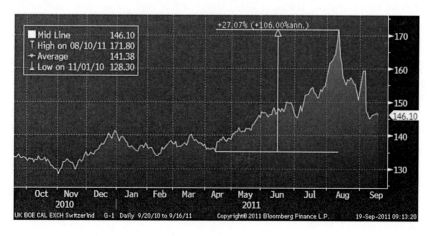

Amid the growing number of near-bankrupt hotels, squeezed exporters and agitated local politicians, the Swiss National Bank (SNB) announced decisive action on 6 September to defend the Swiss economy from this speculative assault:

> "International developments have caused the Swiss franc to appreciate a great deal within a short period of time. This has resulted in a massive overvaluation of our national currency. A massive overvaluation carries the risk of a recession as well as deflationary developments. The Swiss National Bank is therefore aiming for a substantial and sustained weakening of the Swiss Franc. It is prepared to purchase foreign exchange in unlimited quantities".

The key pledge in this declaration is 'to purchase foreign exchange in unlimited quantities'. With its ability to print unlimited amounts of Swissie at zero marginal cost, this is a pledge that the SNB unquestionably has the power to honour.

By this declaration, a central bank widely respected as the linchpin of a successful European economy asserted its willingness and ability to act in the interests of that economy, against an irrational speculative frenzy that it believes poses a grave economic threat.

Since the onset of the Euro-area 'debt crisis', with the exception of the limited 'private sector involvement' options outlined in the second rescue package for Greece, the governments of the area and the European Central Bank have been adamant that the sovereign obligations of all members will be met – all holders of debt issued by member governments can rest assured that that they will be repaid. In the words of the 21 July 2011 statement from the Euro area heads of government and EU institutions:

> "We reaffirm our commitment to the Euro and to do whatever is needed to ensure the financial stability of the Euro area as a whole and its member states. All other (i.e. other than Greece) Euro countries solemnly reaffirm their inflexible determination to honour fully their own individual sovereign signature".

A glance at the bond yields of Ireland, Portugal, Italy or Spain, however, confirms the gaping gap between this commitment from the Euro-area authorities and the collective will of the speculative herd. Just as they have sought to profit by buying the Swissie, they are continuing to profit from their selling of the sovereign bonds of the so-called Euro 'periphery'.

The evidence of the irrationality of the herd in this case is not to be found in the price of burgers under the famous golden arches in Zurich, but in the movement of Irish bond yields in recent weeks. The benchmark two-year yield, for example, hit an annual level of 23% on 18 July 2011 from around 11% at the end of May, and stands a little over 8% today. While there are always those who will supply a supporting narrative to rationalise such gyrations, the most compelling explanation is herd behaviour run riot again.

It is time for the Euro-area authorities, in particular the ECB, to follow the lead of their neighbours across the Alps and to announce their intention to defend their economy. Indeed, borrowing the statement issued by the SNB and making a few small changes would suffice:

> "International developments have caused some Euro area sovereign bond yields to rise markedly in recent times. This has resulted in a massive undervaluation of these bonds. A massive undervaluation carries the risk of a recession as well as deflationary developments. The European Central Bank is therefore aiming for a substantial and sustained appreciation of the sovereign bonds of the so-called Euro 'periphery'. It is prepared to purchase these bonds in unlimited quantities".

As is the case with the SNB, the ability of the ECB to print unlimited amounts of Euro at zero marginal cost unquestionably gives it the power to honour a pledge to 'purchase these bonds in unlimited quantities'. Such a commitment would end the crippling uncertainty dominating the Euro-area, and allow its leaders the space to carefully plan the next stage of fiscal and political integration that the events of recent years clearly make necessary. The citizens of the Euro-area, no less than those of Switzerland, deserve a leadership that will safeguard their interests in the face of the irrational herd. Global leaders from Washington to Beijing are demanding no less. It's time that it was tamed.

19: DEBT CRISIS WILL BE OVER IF EUROPE'S WORD IS ITS BOND

The Sunday Times, 30 October 2011

Although dominating the political, economic and market landscape for almost three years, the 'debt crisis' in the Euro-zone remains remarkably misunderstood. Framed as a morality tale of the prudent being reluctantly forced to pay for the sins of the reckless, with a starring role for bond traders as righteous sheriffs imposing just punishment for the greater good, this 'crisis' has been allowed to needlessly threaten a global calamity.

It is unarguable that reform of the public sector, tax and welfare systems is a necessary, continuing process for countries in the Euro-zone and elsewhere. With no 'price mechanism' to directly prompt this process, the challenge is for policy-makers to have the ability and courage to continually chart a sensible course. In our case, for example, it is clear that the boom-time political decisions in each of these areas have proven unsustainable and are now being modified accordingly. It is equally clear that prudent regulation, particularly of the financial system, is also a necessary process across all countries. Again in our case, for example, the political and regulatory failure to tackle the near trebling in lending by our 'covered' banks between 2002 and 2008 has been a hugely costly one. None of this, however, is either the cause or the solution to the challenge confronting the Euro-zone.

We are in an era of low global inflation, interest rates and bond yields. The noisy barking of 'bond vigilantes', the distracting wrangling of politicians and the token warnings of rating agencies are all irrelevant. Ten-year sovereign bond yields, for example, in the US, the UK and Japan are currently 2.2%, 2.5% and 1.0% respectively (see the graph of the US 10-year yield below).

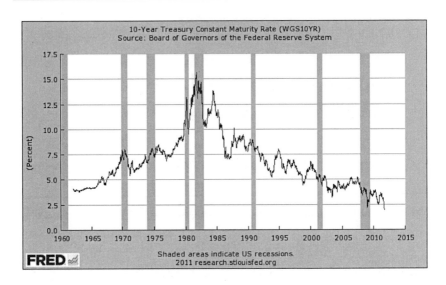

Each of these countries has a debt to GDP ratio and a current budget deficit as a percentage of GDP markedly higher than that for the Euro-zone, and indeed little different to the currently pressured Euro-zone members of Ireland, Portugal, Spain and Italy. Equally, there is no evidence that the efficiency of the public sector, tax and welfare systems, or the successes of regulatory oversight, have shown themselves to be better in the US, the UK and Japan. Yet investors are content to fund these governments at historically-low interest rates, safe in the knowledge that every dollar, pound and yen will be repaid in full and on time.

The process of European integration that began with the coal and steel community in 1951 has been an extraordinary success. A limited association of six members evolved into a broader European Economic Community in 1967, adding three new members in 1973, one in 1981, two in 1986, one in 1995 and 14 in 2004. A union of 27 member states, with 17 sharing a common currency, now stands where rivalry, suspicion and often war was the historic norm. The challenges of post-war reconstruction, Cold War division and Soviet collapse have been successfully overcome. A militarised continent of seething division is now an open, peaceful union of broadly-common values.

It is inconceivable that failure to complete the simple steps now demanded by the logic of a common currency will be allowed to derail the settled, successful policy of over 60 years. The intensifying drama of Franco-German deadlock followed by breakthrough and 'grand bargain' is little more than a distracting charade. There is no Euro-zone 'debt crisis', merely a political challenge to take the next evolutionary step.

This challenge is simply stated. The political leaders of the Euro-zone must now match the assurance of their counterparts in Washington, London and Tokyo. The confusing alphabet soup of ESM and EFSF, the various schemes for 'blue' bonds and 'red' bonds, the misguided rush to re-capitalise banks and the myriad of related suggestions need to give way to finality on this issue. The logic of a common currency demands no less. Those who lend to constituent countries of the Euro-zone must be given complete assurance that they will be repaid in full and on time. They must be assured that the likelihood of this not happening is as negligible as the US, UK or Japanese governments inexplicably deciding not to stand over their equivalent commitments.

Successfully conveyed, which will involve the explicit underlining that the ECB, no less than the Federal Reserve, the Bank of England or the Bank of Japan, has unlimited power to honour bond-holders, this assurance will see the borrowing costs of all constituent countries collapse to that enjoyed by Obama, Cameron and Noda: 'debt' crisis definitively resolved, political challenge successfully overcome. Irish 15-year bonds offering an annual return of around 8% continue to offer compelling value.

20: TROIKA ISN'T STRANGLING US, IT'S OUR SAFETY NET FOR SOVEREIGNTY

The Sunday Times, 20 November 2011

As we move towards Budget day and the chorus of concern about the pain to come from a deficit reduction of €3.8 billion grows louder, imagine the effects if this reduction was suddenly over *five times* bigger? Imagine the impact of such a reduction on our health budget or education, our welfare provision or public sector pay and pensions?

The arrival of the Troika in Ireland almost a year ago was a traumatic event in our history. For the first time, our government was unable to access the funding needed to run the State and had to look to the assistance of others to make up the shortfall. The blow to our national self-esteem and international standing has been severe.

For much of the time since, an angry domestic narrative of an external power imposing unnecessary and unfair austerity on an innocent citizenry has been widespread. Often combined with an aggressive questioning of our membership of the Euro, this story of hapless Irish victims needlessly suffering at the greedy claws of the Troika could not be further from the truth. This is even more the case following the significant positive changes to the terms of our programme announced in July.

The freely-made Irish government decisions of 2000 to 2008 saw government expenditure almost double in real terms (see the graph below from the 2009 article by Governor Honohan, 'What went wrong in Ireland?').

In particular, substantially increased quasi-fixed commitments to public sector employees and to those in receipt of State benefits were made in successive 'partnership' agreements and annual budgets. Unfortunately, the revenue flow underpinning these expenditure commitments proved to be highly correlated to the property market and consequently collapsed. The resulting deficit, and our continuing inability to fund it, is the fundamental reason for the presence of the Troika. Absent their support, we face the immediate and brutal closing of this gap.

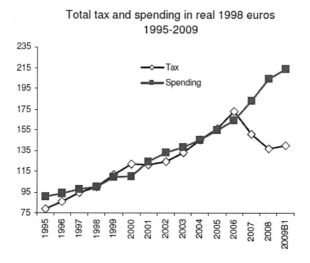

Figure 2: Ireland: Total tax and Government Spending in Real Terms, 1995-2009 (NB: 2009 is the forecast provided in the October 2008 budget statement) Source: CSO: National Income and Expenditure, 2007 and Budget Statement, October 2008.

It is not difficult to imagine how such a development could cause a sudden and dramatic breakdown of much that our society takes for granted. The chaos unleashed in Russia in the immediate aftermath of the Soviet collapse, or Argentina following its default and banishment from capital markets in 2001, give some flavour as to the possible impact on life in Ireland absent the current funding from the Troika. Events in Greece in coming months may yet tragically provide a more up-to-date example. The following quote from a *Financial Times* article by Simon Kuper in July, recalling a 2002 visit to Buenos Aires, chillingly conjures the stark reality faced by many in Argentina a decade ago:

"Every day in Buenos Aires I heard stories of people who had fallen through the trapdoor. There was the former architect who now sold eggs from her kitchen table. There was the 71-year-old once-rich businessman with a second home in the Uruguayan resort of Punta Del Este who was now earning $120 a month as an exterminator. All of these people felt disbelief. This couldn't be happening to them. It turned out that there was no safety net, no benevolent state".

The Troika is our safety net. The funding it provides is keeping us clear of the trapdoor.

A less dramatic way of thinking about this is to consider our position relative to that of Spain and Italy at the moment. We are being funded to at least 2013, with strong indications that this will be extended if required, at an interest rate close to the average that the Troika is paying for our funds. By contrast, Spain and Italy are being funded in the bond market at a substantially higher cost. That this has been negotiated with little rancour from our partners, and that these countries that are facing higher funding costs than us are participating in supporting us, is a remarkable display of solidarity.

While keeping us insulated from the strong likelihood of immediate chaos, the funding from the Troika is crucially affording us the time to close our budget deficit *via* a multi-year programme. The recent confirmation from the Troika, for the third successive quarter, that we are implementing this difficult, but necessary programme is another step along the path to regained sovereignty and national self-esteem.

The misunderstanding, innocent or otherwise, of the Troika mission and what it means for Ireland recalls the story of Samuel Beckett when asked by a French journalist: *"Vous êtes Anglais, Monsieur Beckett?"*. To which Beckett replied: *"Au contraire"*.

The Troika mission in Ireland is not the death-knell of our sovereignty and society, but rather the means by which we can regain the former to the lasting benefit of the latter, following the disastrous myopia of 2000 to 2008.

As the drama in the Euro-zone seems to intensify by the day, we should continue to grab the opportunity presented by this misunderstood mission with both hands – unlike others before us, we are fortunate to have it.

21: CENTRAL BANKS: MAESTRO PUPPETEERS OR KIDS IN THE AUDIENCE?

Value Investment Institute, December 2011

The Great Depression following the Wall Street crash of 1929 has been widely blamed on the flawed policy response of the US Federal Reserve. Most famously, the doyen of monetary economics, Milton Friedman, argued that the collapse of the US Money Supply by a third between 1929 and 1933 turned a brutal day on the stock market into a multi-year depression. In Friedman's view, the failure of the Federal Reserve to maintain the Money Supply caused the vicious cycle of collapsing banks, activity and hope:

> "The Federal Reserve System could have prevented the decline (in the Money Supply) at all times. The terrible depression which followed the crash was a direct result of bungling by the Federal Reserve System".

This view was powerfully endorsed by current Fed Chairman Ben Bernanke in his remarks at Friedman's 90th birthday celebration in 2002:

> "Let me end my talk by abusing slightly my status as an official representative of the Federal Reserve. I would like to say to Milton and Anna: Regarding the Great Depression. You're right, we did it. We're very sorry. But thanks to you, we won't do it again".

Central to the views of Friedman, Bernanke and many others is the assumed ability of the Federal Reserve to determine the Money Supply. In simple terms, as the controller of the dollar printing press, the Federal Reserve is assumed to control the quantity of money in the economy: the Money Supply. In practice, the mechanism by which the Fed is assumed to exercise this control is familiar to all who have had the dubious pleasure of sitting through an economics class on the 'money multiplier'.

Assume that the reserve ratio set by the Fed for the banking system is 10% and assume that the Fed wants to increase the Money Supply by $1,000. They effectively print $100 of notes/'reserves' and use them to buy $100 of US Treasury Bonds on the open market. The seller of the bonds deposits her $100 proceeds at her bank, which puts $10 aside as a reserve and loans out $90 to a customer looking to pay his gas bill. The gas company deposits their $90 proceeds at their bank, which puts $9 aside as a reserve and loans out $81 to a customer looking to go to the opera. The opera company deposits their $81 proceeds at their bank and the process continues until a total of $1,000 in 'new money' has been 'created' i.e. the policy objective of the Fed to increase the Money Supply by $1,000 has been achieved.

Crucial to this story is not the oft-commented-on wonder of the multiplier, but the direction of causation i.e. the Fed determines the Money Supply and we can all rest assured that having learned the lessons of the 1930s, that they have the necessary wisdom and policy levers to avoid a repeat.

Unfortunately, there is an alternative view of how the Money Supply is determined which is so at odds with that of Friedman and Bernanke, that it brings to mind the story of Irish writer Samuel Beckett when asked by a French journalist: "Vous êtes Anglais, Monsieur Beckett?", to which Beckett replied: "Au contraire". In fact, this alternative view of Money Supply determination runs in completely the reverse direction and was summarized well by the Senior Vice President of the New York Fed, Alan Holmes, in 1969:

> "In the real world, banks extend credit, creating deposits in the process, and look for reserves later".

While this view has many implications, its relevance here is that the Fed does not determine the Money Supply. In practice, while they can certainly print dollars / 'reserves' to buy US Treasury Bonds, they have no way of ensuring that this will cause lending into the economy by the banking system.

In Banks we (lack) Trust

The collapse of Lehman Brothers in September 2008 froze the global credit system and threatened to plunge the global economy into a depression. As trust between banks, as well as between banks and their customers, was shaken violently, global trade and activity collapsed in a frightening downward spiral. Many feared that a depression of 1930s dimensions was underway.

The dramatic response of the Fed under Bernanke, no doubt driven by the lessons that he and Friedman had drawn from the Great Depression, has seen the Fed effectively print an unprecedented amount of dollars / 'reserves' to buy an unprecedented amount of US Treasury (and other) Bonds. Under the strange moniker of 'quantitative easing', this response has either been widely praised for having averted a depression, or widely criticised for being an inevitable precursor to runaway inflation. The alternative view is that the Fed is no maestro puppeteer. Stemming from the views of Holmes and others, the Fed's power in determining the Money Supply appears to be far less than conventional wisdom gives them credit. By facilitating the banking system to the degree that it has since the financial crisis begun in earnest in 2008, the Fed likely averted a sharp contraction in the Money Supply. That Money Supply has remained relatively stable over the period is certainly to their credit. However if the demand for money / credit remains moribund, its price (i.e. the interest rate) will remain low. He with a bag of supply tools may be powerless to reverse its decline.

If such a statement sounds too great a departure from the conventional view of the pivotal role of central bank power, the following argument supports the same low rate / yield conclusion from a more conventional perspective. Viewing the ongoing economic malaise as fundamentally a crisis in the modern banking system, the over-riding fear of provoking the 'money destroying monster' will likely lead central bankers to keep rates and yields (and therefore the appropriate discount rate) anchored.

'Money Destroying Monster'

Whatever your view of the why and the how of the collapse of Lehman Brothers almost three years ago, its demise (and the fear that others like it will follow suit) continues to impact trust in the global banking system. Fixing this trust will likely dominate central bank thinking for the foreseeable future. To understand why this is the case, consider a simple example of how a modern bank creates money by granting a loan:

1. A bank grants a loan of €10,000 to a customer to buy a car. The bank credits the current account of the customer, who writes a cheque for €10,000 to the seller of the car.

2. The seller of the car deposits the cheque to her bank account. If this is the same bank as that of the car-buyer, this bank now has an asset in the form of the loan to the car-buyer, funded by a liability in the form of the deposit from the car-seller. Alternatively, if the car-seller deposits the cheque at a different bank, the bank of the car-buyer will borrow €10,000 *via* the inter-bank market to transfer to the bank of the car-seller and, while having the same 'asset' as before, it is now funded in the form of this inter-bank loan.

The net effect of this process is that €10,000 has been created from nothing and is now circulating in the economy. The bank that granted the loan is profiting from charging a higher interest rate to its car-buying customer than it pays to either the car-selling depositor or, in the alternative case, to the inter-bank lender. This profit potential incentivises the bank to repeat the process as often and to the largest extent possible.

The regulatory constraint on this is theoretically two-fold:

1. The bank must fulfil a 'reserve ratio' i.e. it must hold a certain percentage of its liabilities in reserve at the central bank. While in theory this enables the central bank to control the quantum of loans granted by the bank, in practice the central bank must acquiesce to the lending decisions of the bank by ensuring that sufficient reserves are always available for the bank to meet its reserve ratio. In effect, there is no reserve constraint on the bank loaning and thereby creating as much money as it chooses. This reality was summarised well by Canadian economist Basil J. Moore in 1983:

> "Once deposits have been created by an act of lending, the
> central bank must ensure that the required reserves are
> available. Otherwise the banks, no matter how hard they
> scramble for funds, could not in aggregate meet their
> reserve requirements".

2. The bank must also fulfil a 'capital ratio': it must hold a certain
   percentage of capital, such as equity provided by its shareholders, to
   its assets such as loans. While again, in theory, this enables the
   central bank to control the quantum of loans granted by the bank, in
   practice, a bank determined to grant more loans is free to both
   increase its capital via retained profits and / or raise fresh capital
   without any interference from the central bank. In effect, there is little
   'capital' constraint on the bank loaning and thereby creating as much
   money as it chooses.

Now consider the impact of any doubt emerging about the ability or
willingness of the car-buying borrower to repay his loan. Concerned
about the security of their money, the car-selling depositor, or in the
alternative case the inter-bank lender, are likely to seek immediate
repayment from the car-buyer's bank. Unable to seek immediate
repayment from the car-buying borrower, or to source funding
elsewhere as doubt about its loan-book spreads, the bank is forced to
source the funds it needs from the central bank.

This is the predicament of many banks across the Euro-zone
periphery. Widely-voiced doubts about the ability or willingness of their
borrowing customers (individuals or governments) to repay their loans
has sparked a flight of deposits and a recalling of inter-bank loans,
leaving these banks hugely reliant on funding provided by the ECB.

More recently, the possibility that doubt about Euro-zone banks may
impact elsewhere has begun to emerge. Many of the larger Euro-zone
banks, for example, have substantial operations in the United States, and
rumours that they are having difficulty continuing to access the
required dollar funding have grown louder. In particular, it has been
widely reported that a major Euro-zone bank was unable to access a
required $500m in funding earlier this year and was forced to turn to the

ECB. If true, this in turn would have forced the ECB to turn to the Fed to source the required dollars.

It is *via* such a process that the paralyzing infection of doubt, so apparent in many Euro-zone banks, could mutate into a disease that attacks the global banking system. The likely consequences of this are unknowable, as the Nixon-ignited 'money creation' engine of modern banking is potentially shunted into reverse to become a 'money destroying' monster. This potential 'nightmare on main-street' likely unites Bernanke, Draghi and King in sleeplessness. Low interest rates for a long time may be unavoidable.

Of course, this is but one scenario. An alternative one is that confidence in the banking system returns, demand for credit resumes with abandon and the recently printed currency unleashes an inflationary spring far worse than our wildest imaginations.

Intriguingly, highly respected value investors are on opposite sides of this debate. In the blue corner we have Prem Watsa of Fairfax, who has purchased long-term inflation linked instruments that pay off in a deflationary environment (perhaps caused by money destruction). In the red corner we have Seth Klarman of Baupost who is concerned that "the government's fiscal and monetary experiments may go awry, resulting in runaway inflation or currency collapse" – he's been buying gold and other inflation hedges.

The interest rate environment is an important input for investing in all asset classes. The central bank authorities would have us believe that they are in full control of interest rates. This is not necessarily the case.

22: EURO-ZONE NEEDS A NAMA TO SURVIVE

The Sunday Business Post, 24/25 December 2011

The crisis in the Euro-zone shows no sign of abating. Two weeks after the latest EU summit, the prospect of a new fiscal compact, greater ECB intervention and EU treaty change being successfully choreographed to deliver a definitive resolution to the crisis is being met with widespread scepticism.

Crucially, the position of the ECB, as steadfast defender of its independence in the face of multiple calls to follow the lead of its counterparts across the globe and commit to being a lender of last resort, remains effectively unchanged in the eyes of sovereign bond investors. The continuing fear of ultimately not being repaid in full and on time remains undiminished. Investor willingness to fund countries as diverse as Japan, the US and the UK on a 10-year basis at annual interest rates below 2%, safe in the knowledge that their yen, dollars and sterling will be repaid in full and on time, continues to contrast sharply with their scepticism that an equivalent certainty has been constructed for the Euro-zone.

Without delving into the arguments for or against this scepticism, I want to focus on a simple proposal that crucially requires nothing new from the ECB, but nonetheless would ensure the sustainable funding of Euro-zone sovereigns. The space and time needed for European leaders to forge a credible and durable Euro-zone, free from unrelenting market pressure, then would finally be at hand.

After the collapse of Irish property prices and the resulting collapse of confidence in the value of the property-related loan assets of the Irish banks, the government intervened to try to restore confidence in the banking system by setting up NAMA. The lengthy debate about the rights, the wrongs or the mistakes in design of this intervention does not concern me here. My focus is on the key features of the NAMA framework, which with a minor modification can be the basis for a Euro-zone mechanism to sustainably fund Euro-zone sovereigns, without requiring anything new from the ECB. Let's call that mechanism the Euro Asset Management Agency: EURAMA.

The NAMA framework created a new institution, NAMA, which transferred a new asset, NAMA bonds, to the Irish banks in return for an asset in which confidence had collapsed – the property-related loan assets of the Irish banks. The two key features of relevance in this framework are:

- The risk to the future value of the property-related loan assets is borne by NAMA;
- The ECB accepts NAMA bonds as collateral to secure funding at the ECB refinancing rate – currently 1%.

The balance sheet of NAMA is thus:

NAMA - Balance Sheet

Assets	Liabilities
Property-related loan assets	NAMA bonds

In equivalent fashion, the EURAMA framework would create a new institution, EURAMA, which would transfer a new asset, EURAMA bonds, to the holders of Euro-zone sovereign bonds (including the ECB) in return for said Euro-zone sovereign bonds. The modification in comparison to NAMA is that the Euro-zone sovereign bonds are transferred to EURAMA at par to reflect the zero risk of default (excluding Greece), as definitively promised at the recent EU summit when so-called 'private sector involvement' was explicitly ruled out. The two key features of relevance in this framework would be:

- The risk to the future value of the Euro-zone sovereign bonds (definitively put at zero at the recent summit – excluding Greece) would be borne by EURAMA;
- The ECB would accept EURAMA bonds as collateral to secure funding at the ECB refinancing rate – currently 1%.

The balance sheet of EURAMA would thus be:

EURAMA - Balance Sheet

Assets	Liabilities
Euro-zone sovereign bonds	EURAMA bonds

The stock of outstanding Euro-zone sovereign bonds likely to be transferred to EURAMA would have an average duration of around seven years. With the borrowing needs of these governments also to be met for, say, the next three years *via* this mechanism, in a further echo of NAMA, the expected life of EURAMA also would be about 10 years. EURAMA then could be wound down without cost to the pocket of any taxpayer or the existing independence of the ECB.

The continuing high borrowing costs faced by sovereign borrowers across the Euro-zone compared to their counterparts in Japan, the US and elsewhere, reflects the extent to which sovereign bond investors remain sceptical of being repaid in full and on time by many Euro-zone sovereign borrowers. The continuing reluctance of the ECB to definitively address this scepticism for fear of compromising its independence demands an alternative intervention: an intervention designed to overcome the former without damaging the latter.

The model for such an intervention, which crucially requires nothing new from the ECB, has existed in Ireland for almost three years. The logjam between what the Euro-zone needs and what the ECB is prepared to deliver can be broken. The NAMA framework, with minor modification, can become a EURAMA framework to break the logjam paralysing the Euro-zone.

While I accept that almost everything that has happened since the onset of the crisis makes such an intervention unlikely, I still think it's important to tease out how it could happen without requiring anything new from the independence-obsessed ECB. Despite the obvious counter-arguments of those, in particular, who view bond markets as all-knowing, I believe that Europe can now benefit from looking to Ireland: the Euro-zone needs a NAMA.

23: THE CHALLENGE OF VALUE INVESTING

The Sunday Business Post, 12 February 2012

The choice of a discount rate to assess the value of an asset is an unavoidable challenge for every investor. In tandem with a reasonable assessment of the likely sustainable earnings-flow on offer to the potential asset holder at the current price, it is the crucial pre-requisite to deciding whether an asset should be bought or not.

To give a little context to this challenge, it may be helpful to consider a number of the approaches that have been/continue to be used:

- The father of value investing, Ben Graham, chose a simple formula that incorporated his assessment of the sustainable earnings of the asset in question, the likely growth of these earnings and the yield offered by the 30-year AAA corporate bond index;

- The approach of his most famous and successful student, Warren Buffett, is even simpler and was summarised well in this quote from his letter to the shareholders of Berkshire Hathaway in 1998:

  "We don't discount the future cash flows at 9% or 10%; we use the US treasury rate. We try to deal with things about which we are quite certain. You can't compensate for risk by using a high discount rate."

- The adherents of the efficient markets hypotheses (EMH), and its logical extension the capital asset pricing model (CAPM), which have dominated both campus and trading room in recent decades, approach this issue with a formula that looks to incorporate a 'risk free' rate and an 'equity risk premium' (ERP): Discount Rate = Risk Free Rate + ERP.

While there are many points of debate about each of these approaches and the many variations of them, the key point of relevance here is that they all implicitly or explicitly incorporate the use of an 'interest rate' believed to be at or close to 'risk free'.

The question I want to consider is how credible or sustainable is the continued use by many investors of a discount rate of 8% or higher – which incorporates a 'risk free rate' assumed to be 5% to 6% – in an era when interest rates and bond yields are at multi-decade lows and have been in structural decline since Reagan first won the White House (see graph below).

While debate about the sustainability of such historically-low interest rates and bond yields rages loudly, I think that there are at least two strong arguments for believing that no significant reversal of this trend is on the horizon:

- Having cut the price of short-term money to almost zero and bought substantial quantities of Treasury bonds, many believe that the Federal Reserve is now all but impotent in determining the money supply. They believe that, contrary to the views of Friedman and his most famous student Bernanke, the continuing lack of demand for credit renders the Fed effectively powerless to meaningfully reverse the de-leveraging forces dominating the economy or the current level of bond yields;

- If such a statement sounds overly definite and too great a departure from the conventional view of central bank power, consider instead the view that the 'crisis' of the last three years is fundamentally a crisis in the modern banking system. With its heightened potential to reverse from being a 'money-creating engine' into a 'money-destroying monster', Bernanke, Draghi and King are set to keep the price of money as low as possible for as long as possible to cushion the banking system as much as possible.

The choice of discount rate is an essential and unavoidable decision in the valuing of an asset. Everything else being equal, the higher the rate, the lower the value and *vice versa*. A key ingredient in the calculation of an 'appropriate' discount rate is the rate on offer from a broadly 'risk free' alternative. Once again, the lower this rate is assumed to be on a sustainable basis, the higher the value and *vice versa*.

Interest rates and broad 'risk free' yields have been in a generally declining trend since 1981, and are currently at lows not seen in over 50 years. The forces of central bank impotence and/or fear need to be considered in this context.

In the same context, is the consensus choice of discount rate by many investors something that needs re-thinking? Would this in turn imply a re-rating of assets such as stocks and property? Or, alternatively, will investors continue for the foreseeable future to hoard their cash waiting for 'rates' to return to some perceived 'normality'?

24: FOLLOWING THE HERD CAN BE A DANGEROUS GAME

The Sunday Times, 19 February 2012

The Nobel committee deciding on the 2002 award of the Memorial Prize in Economics chose to break with tradition by awarding the prize to a psychologist: Daniel Kahneman.

Primarily for his seminal paper with Amos Tversky in 1974, 'Judgement under Uncertainty: Heuristics and Biases', the award was an acknowledgement of how the work of Kahneman and Tversky had powerfully shaken the key assumptions underpinning classical economics. In particular, their compelling portrayal of human decision-making as being littered with systematic short-cuts and biases casts great doubt over the key assumption of 'rationality' and has helped to spark new fields of 'behavioural' enquiry in economics, finance and elsewhere.

Unfortunately, such enquiry has been largely confined to the margins, with mainstream economics remaining comfortably under the blanket of its conventional assumptions. As one of many examples, consider this quote from another esteemed winner of the Memorial Prize, Paul Krugman, who was clearly so convinced about the ability of 'rationally' applied policy to 'rationally' guide economic outcomes that he said in 1997:

> "If you want a simple model for predicting the unemployment rate in the United States over the next few years, here it is: It will be what Greenspan wants it to be, plus or minus a random error reflecting the fact that he is not quite God".

Unsurprisingly, a further example of the continued mainstream adherence to the assumption of 'rationality' is the subject of the quote from Krugman. In the wake of the collapse of Lehman Brothers in

September 2008, the legendary Chairman of the Federal Reserve Alan Greenspan underlined his own (now severely shaken) belief in the efficacy of the assumption of rationality when he admitted:

> "Those of us who have looked to the self-interest of lending institutions to protect shareholders' equity – myself especially – are in a state of shocked disbelief".

It is clearly a slow process, even for Nobel winners, to convince long-standing believers to question a key assumption underpinning their conventional view of the world. However, the global financial crisis of recent years and the failure of mainstream thinking to provide satisfying explanations have intensified the doubts raised by Kahneman and others. A richer understanding of the forces that can cause such a crisis is clearly needed. In this respect, Kahneman and his work on decision-making and its systematic biases offer much material. It is no surprise that his recent book *Thinking Fast and Slow*, summarising a lifetime of investigating these forces, has become a global phenomenon.

In that context, I also want to highlight the insights of the economist Andrew Oswald of Warwick University – insights that I believe are of particular relevance to investors.

In a speech to the London School of Economics last November ploughing a different, if related, furrow to Kahneman, 'Herd Behaviour and Keeping up with the Joneses', Oswald outlined the key insight of how individual rationality often can be consistent with collective catastrophe.

Taking his lead from the animal kingdom, Oswald argues that, because human happiness is a function of relative rather than absolute position within a group, herding or clustering behaviour is the rational response of the vast majority of individuals to the vast majority of situations. With a range of examples from fashion to frogs, he makes a compelling case that humans are frightened of falling behind and consequently are prompted to constantly adjust their relative position within a group just as an animal seeking safety will do in a herd.

As with the herd, however, this individually-rational behaviour on occasion can lead to collective catastrophe. The stark image from Thomas Hardy of the flock of sheep plunging to their collective deaths, rationally following each other over the cliff-side to maintain their relative position, has profound real-world implications.

Oswald uses the following graph of the real price of US housing from 1892 to 2010 to show how such individually-rational but herd-like behaviour can lull many into ignoring objective evidence and plunging to collective catastrophe. As this country knows to its continuing cost, the equivalent graph here would look even more dramatic.

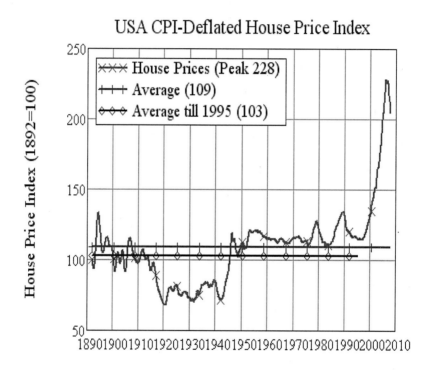

Some of the lessons for the investor are clear:

- Succumbing to the powerful instinct, however individually rational, to maintain relative position in a charging investment herd is inviting catastrophe;

- The striking success of value investing – maintaining the discipline only to buy assets below a reasonable assessment of their true worth – as memorably extolled by its most successful practitioner Warren Buffett in his article 'The Super-Investors of

Graham and Doddsville' is more richly understood by reference to the work of Oswald on the powerful herding instinct of humans;

- However, if you must seek comfort in an investment herd, at least make sure it is one populated by the followers of the Sage of Omaha – if you can't resist it, try to make the herding instinct of millennia work in your favour!

25: THE NUMBER'S UP FOR FLAWED RISK FORMULA

The Sunday Times, 25 March 2012

The disappointing returns produced by conventional investment products over the last decade have seen a proliferation of alternatives holding out the prospect of a better outcome. From various multi-asset strategies to so-called absolute return funds, Irish investors now are being offered a wide range of products purporting to deliver a superior investment experience to that offered by conventional managed or equity funds. Domestic fund-flows bear out the success of these alternatives in attracting a growing proportion of investment.

While greater choice is always to be welcomed, I believe a common worrying feature of many of these offerings needs to be highlighted: the key assumption that risk is a quantitative concept that can be successfully measured and managed.

There are many examples of how pervasive this dangerous assumption has become now in the products being assessed and offered here. Definitions of 'absolute return funds', such as that from the European Securities and Markets Authority as "funds managed ... under the constraint of a pre-determined risk limit", have gained wide currency. A clear acceptance of the worrying assumption that risk is a quantitative concept that can be successfully measured and managed is now widespread. It is beyond time to raise the red flag of warning to those being tempted into such products.

There is no doubt that dealing with risk is a constant challenge facing every investor. The challenge of how to sensibly assess the future remains central to any investment decision. It is both unsurprising and right that one of the most common questions asked by investment consultants and prospective investors to investment managers everywhere is "How do you manage risk?". The answer to this question should always be fundamental to any decision they make to part with hard-earned cash.

This challenge is hardly a new one. The American investor and economic historian Peter L. Bernstein, in his 1996 book, *Against the Gods: The Remarkable Story of Risk*, gives a particularly engaging account of how the great minds of philosophy, science and mathematics have grappled with this issue down the ages. Beginning with the numbering systems of the ancient east and touching on the work of famed figures such as Pascal, Bernoulli, Bayes and Galton, Bernstein concludes that the breakthrough of Markowitz in the 1950s, followed by Merton, Black and Scholes in the 1970s has freed mankind from the dark shadows of ignorance. With barely concealed excitement, he concludes that the tools to successfully master risk are finally to hand:

> "The revolutionary idea that defines the boundary between modern times and the past is the mastery of risk".

The impact of this methodology on banks, investment funds and regulators around the globe was profound. In practice, it seemed that trading exposure across a wide range of markets, assets and instruments now could be expressed in a single number. A simple aggregation of the relative historic price volatilities of the various positions seemingly sufficed as a comprehensive measure of risk. Easy to calculate and understand, this quantification, measurement and management of risk gained rapid acceptance across the financial world.

In 1994, Merton and Scholes joined the legendary John Meriwether of Salomon Brothers to form the (in)famous hedge fund, Long Term Capital Management (LTCM). Their mastery of risk now would be exploited in the hunt for return. Three years of annualised returns touching 40% followed, as did the award of the 1997 Nobel Prize in Economics. The ascendency of their approach – the calculation of a number *via* a simple mathematical formula – to mastering risk seemed assured. The excitement of Bernstein and the global fame of Merton and Scholes seemed fully justified.

Nine months after the triumph of the Nobel Prize in Stockholm, LTCM crashed spectacularly. All of its investors were wiped out and the reverberations of its collapse were felt globally. While its extensive use of leverage played a key role, it's also clear that the seemingly unshakeable quantitative models on which the firm was founded had crumbled in the face of the Russian default. The measurement and management of risk proved not so amenable to modelling after all.

The lesson drawn from this catastrophic collapse, however, was not the banishment of quantitative efforts to measure and manage risk, but rather their further elaboration to allegedly deal with 'stress' events such as the Russian default. As perceptively put by George Soros:

> "The situation is reminiscent of the French construction of the Maginot Line after the First World War to prepare for static trench warfare; but in the Second World War they were confronted by mobile warfare with tanks".

These prophetic words from 1998 were subsequently vindicated in dramatic fashion as the latest quantitative techniques to measure and manage risk made a major contribution to the global financial crisis of recent years.

The message for the Irish investor is a simple one. Lured by false sirens such as technology stocks and commercial property in recent times, they should now be wary of any product claiming to be able to measure and manage risk. With due regard to the world of elaborate mathematical models, in the real world risk is never a number. As memorably put by Albert Einstein:

> "Not everything that can be counted counts and not everything that counts can be counted".

The great investors from Keynes to Buffett showed a great understanding of this. Trying to understand the approach of these giants and others to this age-old challenge is where I believe we should be focused.

26: NEVER MIND THE INVESTMENT GURUS – BUFFETT IS YOUR MAN

The Sunday Times, 22 April 2012

Open any newspaper, visit any bookshop, tune in to any radio or TV station, and the soothing words of the market pundit predicting 'the next big thing' is impossible to avoid. Economic growth, inflation and interest rates, indeed the direction of every financial variable imaginable, are predicted with plausible-sounding stories as each investment guru seeks to outdo the other in the race to be the champion soothsayer for the period ahead. I wish them all well.

However, before jumping to any investment decisions based on such confidently pronounced forecasts, it may be worth taking a minute or two to ponder the following graph from James Montier of GMO.

Economists Can't Forecast for Toffee (US GDP % YoY)

Source: Federal Reserve Bank of Philadelphia   Actual data through Jun 2010; projection through Sep 2011

According to Montier, the shockingly poor record of economists in forecasting growth, inflation, stock prices or indeed any financial or economic variable you care to mention has 'made astrologers look like professionals'. Having failed to forecast every recession over the last 40 years, the only interesting question when contemplating economists and their forecasts is why anyone still gives them a hearing.

By contrast, it might be more profitable to consider briefly some of the time-worn principles of value investing that continue to underpin the investment approach of many consistently successful investors around the world. Principles they have shown commitment to applying successfully, year in and year out, deaf to the cacophony of predictions competing around them.

To give a little flavour of such an approach, consider some of the core beliefs from just the introduction and the first chapter of the classic *Margin of Safety* by the legendary founder of The Baupost Group, Seth Klarman – a book highly recommended to all interested in investing:

- There is nothing esoteric about value investing. It is simply the process of determining the value underlying a security and then buying it at a considerable discount from that value;

- A margin of safety is necessary because valuation is an imprecise art, the future is unpredictable, and investors are human and do make mistakes;

- In reality, no one knows what the market will do; trying to predict it is a waste of time, and investing based on that prediction is a speculative undertaking;

- Value in relation to price, not price alone, must determine your investment decisions;

- US government securities are generally regarded as 'risk-free' investments … To achieve current cash yields appreciably above those available from US government securities, investors must either risk the loss of principal or incur its certain depletion;

- Despite the enormous effort put into devising (investment) formulas, none has been proven to work. Moreover, if any successful investment formula could be devised, it would be exploited by those who possessed it until competition eliminated the excess profits;

- Investors would be much better off to redirect the time and effort committed to devising formulas into fundamental analysis of specific investment opportunities.

There are no simple rules to consistent investment success, no simple stories that consistently predict the future of financial markets, and no gains attainable beyond the 'risk-free' without an exposure to potential loss.

The only investment approach that has consistently achieved investment success is that based on the principles of value investing. If the Klarman book looks a bit long, browse a copy of 'The Super-investors of Graham and Doddsville', a short 1984 article by a certain Warren E. Buffett.

You will enjoy the read and it will likely save you money – two forecasts that I am happy to stand over!

27: CONFLICTING THEORIES AND IRELAND

The Sunday Business Post, 29 April 2012

Shortly after the collapse of Lehman Brothers and the intensification of the global financial crisis in September 2008, Queen Elizabeth opened a new building at the London School of Economics. Amid the gathered dignitaries, including some world-renowned economists, she famously asked the question about the dramatic financial and economic collapse dominating headlines across the world:

"This is awful. Why did nobody see it coming?".

In response to her question, the British Academy convened a forum the following June of 'experts from business, the City, its regulators, academia and government' and summarised their answer to the Queen in a letter to Buckingham Palace a month later. Far from answering the question, however, this letter is more an example of the extent of the confusion that has gripped the economics profession since the onset of the crisis than a satisfactory explanation of what has happened and why.

From devoted believers in the free market to those who see themselves as the inheritors of the Keynesian mantle of government intervention, the greatest economic crisis since the great depression has been a profound challenge. The size of this challenge can be glimpsed in the following statement from the Nobel laureate in Economics Robert Lucas in the more relaxed days of 2003:

"My thesis in this lecture is that macroeconomics in its original sense has succeeded: its central problem of depression has been solved, for all practical purposes, and has in fact been solved for many decades".

There are few voices in politics, economics or more generally who would agree with such a statement today. A cacophony of competing theories has replaced the comfortable consensus of the pre-crisis period. Take your pick from a German emphasis on government finances to an Anglo-Saxon focus on reviving demand to a variety of lesser highlighted alternatives.

Looking at the current confusion, it is no exaggeration to paraphrase Captain Boyle and say that:

"The economics profession's in a terrible state of chassis".

A recent example of this, with particular relevance to the debate here in Ireland, is the dispute that has broken out between another Nobel laureate Paul Krugman and the lesser known Australian economist, Steve Keen.

Sparked by a paper presented by Keen in Berlin last month, in which he effectively accuses Krugman of misunderstanding how money is created in a modern economy, this dispute is far from an esoteric spat between two academics with strong opinions.

In fact, although neither man references any country in particular, I believe their dispute raises key questions about what drove the boom in Ireland and who bears responsibility for the devastating bust.

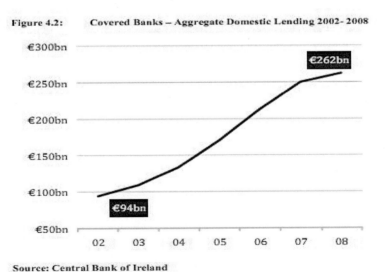

Figure 4.2:   Covered Banks – Aggregate Domestic Lending 2002- 2008

Source: Central Bank of Ireland

The Krugman view supports a narrative of what happened here that has wide domestic acceptance. An unsustainable credit boom was generated by the savings of thrifty core European savers, hunting for higher returns, being loaned by their banks to eager Irish banks and their customers. A near trebling in the outstanding stock of borrowing and lending by Irish banks in the six years to 2008 was the extraordinary outcome (see the graph above from the *Nyberg Report*).

When the loans to the Irish borrowers turned sour, the thrifty European savers and their banks were repaid by the Irish taxpayer with funds borrowed from the ECB, the Irish Central Bank and the Troika. This burden on the Irish taxpayer, crucially generated in the first instance by core savers hunting higher returns, is now viewed by many here as 'odious' and morally indefensible.

By contrast, Keen outlines a process by which private banks determine the money supply. They grant the loans that create the deposits and subsequently secure the required regulatory reserves. It is a process where the money supply effectively is determined by the private banking system, not the central bank, free of any reserve constraint and subject only to an arbitrary and generally easy-to-satisfy (in good times) capital requirement.

The Senior Vice President of the New York Fed, Alan Holmes, summarised this perspective as long ago as 1969:

> "In the real world, banks extend credit, creating deposits in the process, and look for reserves later".

In the Irish case then, the chain was not begun by thrifty savers in the core hunting for higher returns, but by the borrowing and lending decisions of Irish borrowers and private Irish banks. This is the exact reversal of the process argued by Krugman and widely accepted in Ireland.

If Keen is right and his depiction of 'money creation' is correct, many in Ireland are following a false narrative. Our boom and bust was not generated by greedy core savers hunting for higher returns, but by private Irish banks granting loans and creating deposits from thin air in a recklessly-accelerated hunt for profit.

As the world continues to grapple with the many conflicting economic theories now fogging the landscape and the Queen is kept waiting for a more satisfactory answer to her question, it might be time in Ireland to devote some thought to this recent US *v* Australia tussle. We might finally demand a comprehensive explanation of the actions taken by some here, and the inactions of others, in the ruinous six years to 2008.

28: FISCAL TREATY: THE LONGER VIEW

Business & Finance, May/June 2012

A great deal of the commentary on the Euro-zone 'debt crisis' understandably has focused on economic and financial questions – for example: Is economic growth being choked by austerity? What combination of debt-load, funding cost and growth rate is needed to stabilise sovereign debt?

A lot of time has been devoted also to discussion of the short-term political context – for example: What role are looming elections in Greece, France and then Germany playing in the seemingly endless inter-governmental wrangling? Will the referendum in Ireland on the Fiscal Compact be passed? If not, what could be the consequences?

The longer view offered by history has been largely ignored. In particular, consider Europe in the spring of 1914. For the majority of those living there, the prospect of continued social and economic progress must rarely have seemed so secure. Almost a century after the fall of Napoleon and the end of continent-wide conflict, Europe was still a settled and broadly stable polity overseen by six seemingly rational and pragmatic powers. Global trade, industrial expansion and social mobility were accelerating rapidly, as the fruits of historic progress in science, communications and mass production were bringing undreamt of prosperity to ever greater numbers of people.

The political leaders in London, Berlin, Paris, Vienna, Moscow and Istanbul, all seemed to have a deep understanding of the general benefits flowing from a generally stable political landscape. The dominant culture informing the relationships between the great powers remained that of the 'Concert of Europe': the framework of balance and stability initially constructed by arch realist Von Metternich in Vienna in 1815.

The shocking news from Sarajevo on 28 June that the heir to the Austrian throne had been assassinated by a Bosnian-Serb nationalist was an undoubted challenge to this calm political landscape. To contemporary observers, a potential dispute between an understandably upset Austria and an unfortunately vulnerable Serbia clearly had the potential to damage relations across the continent. The political skill that had successfully steered Europe along a broadly peaceful and prosperous path for the previous 99 years, notwithstanding periodic disputes, would be needed once again.

The consensus opinion that it was obviously in the interests of all concerned to achieve a peaceful accommodation looked unarguable. A minor and unexpected problem in a province in south-east Europe would have little general impact. Speaking at the time, the British statesman and writer Henry Noel Brailsford, as quoted by Niall Ferguson in *The Ascent of Money*, summarised this consensus well:

> "In Europe the epoch of conquest is over, it is as certain as anything in politics that the frontiers of our national states are finally drawn. My own belief is that there will be no more wars among the six great powers".

Instead of the calm leadership and political skill generally expected, however, the people of Europe were cursed by a series of disastrous political missteps that led them to catastrophe. The steady, long-sighted calculation of previous decades was swamped by the furious short-sightedness of populist emotion. Across Europe, jingoistic populations were not led maturely away from their worst instincts, but rather encouraged recklessly in their delusional senses of grievance. The collective failure of political leadership shattered decades of general peace and plunged much of the continent into a conflict of unimagined destruction.

When the dust finally settled on an exhausted continent after four years of pointless carnage, the centuries-old rule of the Hapsburgs, Hohenzollerns, Romanovs and Ottomans lay in ruins. Austria-Hungary, Germany, Russia and Turkey were unrecognisable shells, stalked by revolution, dismemberment and hunger. The pyrrhic victors in Britain and France were bankrupt and barely recognisable shadows of their former selves. The price of myopic political leadership indulging short-term domestic emotion had proven to be incalculably high.

The lesson for the leaders of Europe today is a simple one. Like their predecessors in 1914, they can choose to court short-term local popularity by trying to satisfy the narrow demands of angry domestic constituents and risk catastrophe, or they can choose to forge a durable framework of economic, financial and political stability. Recent months suggest a strong determination to follow the latter path and to not permit an unexpected but minor problem, sparked in a south-east corner of our continent, to unleash general chaos again.

As we in Ireland embark on an intensive period of commemoration of the crucial decade of 1912 to 1922, we should reflect on the broader lessons of these pivotal years in Europe. Hovering over our ballot paper in the polling booth on 31 May, we should vote a calm and confident 'Yes' to the evolving European future and our position at its heart. History demands it.

29: GERMANS STILL HAUNTED BY NIGHTMARE INFLATION OF 1920s

The Sunday Times, 24 June 2012

The Euro-zone crisis has been a compelling story. The heightened market volatility, the succession of political summits and the long list of possible policy initiatives all have provided rich material to be assessed and dissected.

While most of this discussion has been characterised by as much confusion and disagreement as the crisis itself, one point of consensus has been widespread: if only the stubborn stance of Germany could be softened, a solution would finally be to hand.

The White House, Downing Street and many governments across the Euro-zone, including our own, seem convinced that German intransigence is unnecessarily prolonging the crisis. This consensus is shared by many of the citizens of these countries who unfortunately have lost their jobs or are struggling to meet higher tax bills from reduced incomes. If only Chancellor Merkel would agree to some mechanism that would substantially ease the burden of individual, bank and sovereign debtors. If only she would follow Fed Chairman Bernanke and Bank of England Governor King and effectively authorise unlimited 'money' creation. All then could return to normal. Or so this consensus asserts.

Yet the recent failure of Spain, following the previous failure of Ireland, to shift the liabilities of its banks to a common European entity highlights once again that Germany does not share this viewpoint. For good or ill, the magical easing of debt burdens and the authorising of unlimited 'money' creation is not the German way. Instead of railing against this perceived stubbornness, it might be better to try and understand it.

The two key uses of 'money' are as a means of exchange and as a store of value. Through history, many items as unlikely to us as seashells and tally-sticks have been used to fulfil these 'money' functions. By the late 19th century, much of the world had followed the example of Britain and adopted the gold standard. This was effectively re-established at Bretton Woods in 1944 and remained in place until 1971. The 'money' of 44 countries was tied to the US dollar, which in turn was anchored to gold at $35 per ounce.

Since the breaking of the link to gold, 'paper money' backed by the promises of the relevant sovereign state/government is the norm. Sterling is backed by the promise of the UK government, the dollar by the US government, the yen by that of Japan and so on. While all of these countries have succeeded in maintaining their respective currencies as an effective means of exchange, there has been a marked difference in their attitude to the second key use of 'money': as a store of value.

Sterling to DM 1971 to 2012

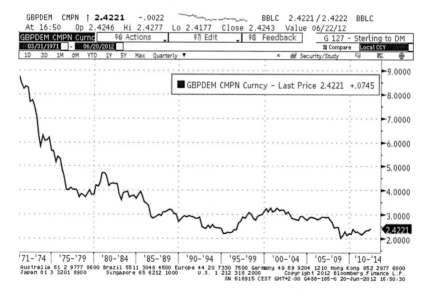

For example, on the night that Nixon shut the gold window in August 1971 and the era of 'paper money' began, £1 sterling bought over 8.5

deutschmarks. By September 1992, the UK government famously failed to maintain a rate of £1 sterling to 2.95 deutschmarks and was forced out of the exchange rate mechanism of the EMS. Today, £1 sterling buys the equivalent of about 2.4 deutschmarks. In half a lifetime, sterling has lost over 70% of its purchasing power relative to the German currency. The German attitude to the store of value function of 'money' has clearly been very different to their neighbours across the North Sea.

To understand why this has been and continues to be the case, consider the following quote from a recent book by the Capital Markets Editor of the *Economist*, Philip Coggan:

> "In 1914, the dollar was worth 4.2 marks. After the war, the dollar was worth 65 marks. In the early 1920s, to avoid the unpopularity of raising taxes or cutting expenditure, the government asked the Reichsbank (the Central Bank) to print the money to cover its deficit. The Reichsbank duly obliged. By August 1923, a dollar could buy 620,000 marks, and by November 630 billion".

In a world of 'paper money', the store of value function of money can be destroyed. The experience of this suffered by the German people within living memory was devastating. Financial ruin was followed by economic collapse and, ultimately, military defeat. Their lack of trust in easy-sounding solutions to the current crisis should be of little surprise. Their lack of enthusiasm for policies that might undermine the value of their 'money' should be seen in this light.

The choice facing the non-German members of the Euro-zone is becoming clearer. We can have a 'paper money' regime that cares little for 'money' as a store of value, or we can have a 'paper money' regime that will continue to include Germany. But we are unlikely to be able to have both. Notwithstanding their recent election result, the first country to have to make this choice looks likely to be Greece. Given the unswerving attachment of Germany to the role of 'money' as a store of value, Greece is unlikely to be last.

30: THE GERMANS HAVE TURNED THE TIDE IN OUR ECONOMIC WATERLOO

The Sunday Times, 22 July 2012

The short communiqué released by the leaders of the Euro-zone in the aftermath of their recent summit has sparked a huge reaction. From the new role envisaged for the ESM to the possible impact on Irish debt sustainability, there has been much debate about its possible implications for a wide range of issues.

Instead of adding to the debate about such issues, I'd like to address what the communiqué means for the money in our pocket.

The history of Europe can be viewed as a series of key moments leading to the current arrangement of States and institutions. The key moments were often military clashes where the outcome was finely balanced. For example, imagine how different the development of our continent might have been if Von Blucher had not arrived to buttress Wellington at Waterloo, or if the Red Army had buckled before the onset of the Russian winter at Stalingrad?

Such key moments have not been confined to military battles. Think of the Europe that might have emerged if Anglo-French thinking at Versailles had been more like US thinking at Bretton Woods, or if Gorbachev had followed the Soviet play-book of 1956 and 1968 when faced with the convulsions of 1989?

The decisive impact that key moments have had in shaping our history is of more than academic interest. It reminds us with sometimes chilling evidence that our future often has been shaped by a key moment, a crucial turning point from which subsequent events can be traced. I believe that the recent European summit will be remembered as such a moment.

The Nobel laureate Paul Krugman cut to the heart of the crisis facing the Euro-zone in a recent interview on the BBC *Newsnight* programme:

"Something impossible is going to happen. One is that the Euro will be allowed to collapse. The other is that Germany will accept lots of debt relief plus inflation plus temporarily large open-ended lending. One of these two impossible things is going to happen".

I believe that the key message of the recent summit is that the latter 'impossibility' has happened. There may have been no explicit mention of 'debt relief plus inflation plus temporarily large open-ended lending', but Germany received sufficient re-assurance to make the decision that the Euro will not be allowed to collapse. Those that doubt German capacity to implement this decision should recall some recent history across the Atlantic.

In the wake of the collapse of Lehman Brothers in September 2008, the US economy and banking system faced collapse. The scale of 'bad debt' throughout its traumatised financial system seemed likely to overwhelm it, and to undermine significantly the leading position of the United States in the world. This view failed to reckon with the powerful levers available to US policy-makers that were used subsequently as the dominant imperative of safeguarding US relative power trumped everything else.

Of most relevance, the Federal Reserve (the US Central Bank) embarked upon a determined policy of purchasing large quantities of distressed mortgage-backed securities, US Treasury bonds and other assets, effectively with dollars it printed for this purpose. Though unconventional and risky, the goal of protecting the US in the global pecking order was just too important to be left to orthodoxy and market forces.

The same is now true of the Euro-zone. So while the details of the summit agreement have yet to be finalised and, no doubt, will be subject to fierce negotiation in coming months, we now can be confident of the following:

- The Euro will survive;
- Depositors in Euro-zone banks are safe;
- Investors in the sovereign debt of peripheral Euro-zone states will be repaid.

The vexed question facing many across Ireland and elsewhere of how to protect their savings finally has been answered. The rush into German, Swiss or other so-called 'safe havens' now can be safely reversed. Germany has made the historic decision that maintaining the Euro is its overarching goal. Another key moment in European history has taken a decisive turn. All else is now detail.

31: THE EURO OUTLOOK – WHAT DOESN'T KILL YOU MAKES YOU STRONGER

The Sunday Times, 16 December 2012

Much of the commentary on the Euro-zone crisis has a noisy immediacy. Market turmoil, competing 'solutions' and high-wire summitry understandably generates a cacophony of clashing opinions, as predictions ranging from the imminent break-up of the single currency to its definitive survival tend to dominate headlines and analysis. By ignoring this short-term frenzy, I think an important insight is now clear for investors willing to take a longer view.

Foreign exchange markets are notoriously unpredictable. Trade flows, capital flows, current and prospective interest rate differences, and a range of other factors combine to drive exchange rates in unknowable directions. There is no evidence that anyone or any system has a sustainable edge in predicting their movement. I have no idea what the Euro/$ exchange rate will be next week, next month or next year. However, at rare moments, I believe a foreign exchange rate view with strong conviction can be expressed and that we are currently at such a moment:

> The Euro will be significantly stronger relative to the dollar at the end of this decade than it is today.

The dollar has dominated the global monetary system since at least the Bretton Woods agreement of 1944. Indeed, many convincingly argue that it replaced sterling as the most important global currency in the mid 1920s – a mere decade after the establishment of the Federal Reserve System and determined efforts by Washington to promote a global role for the greenback.

Whatever your position on the timing of its ascent, there is no debate that the US bestrode the global economy in the aftermath of World War II. It accounted for almost half of global output and was the largest importer, provider of trade credit, source of foreign capital around the world and the ultimate anchor of the Bretton Woods system.

The consequent dominance of the dollar was unchallenged and looked unchallengeable. So dominant in fact that the risky decision by Nixon of breaking with gold and effectively collapsing Bretton Woods in the early 1970s did little to dim the allure of the dollar. Equally, neither the inflationary excesses of the decade that followed nor the extraordinary Fed policy of recent years has altered the dollar's pre-eminent position.

For almost a century now, it has been the lynchpin of the global monetary system and has enjoyed what was evocatively described as 'an exorbitant privilege' by then French Finance Minister Giscard D'Estaing as long ago as 1965.

Over 60% of global central bank reserves are still held in dollars today. Nearly 50% of global debt issuance is in dollars. All commodities of any economic consequence, most importantly oil, are priced in dollars and 85% of all foreign exchange transactions involve the dollar. The dollar still dominates the invoicing and settling of international transactions between many countries other than the United States.

The reason for the continuance of this 'exorbitant privilege' can no longer be the dominance of the US economy. After all, the US share of global exports has now fallen to 13%, and it is now the source of less than 20% of foreign direct investment, compared to almost 85% between 1945 and 1980. More worryingly for Washington, the US has gone from being the biggest creditor nation on the globe to its biggest debtor over the last decade and a half.

No, the fundamental reason is simply the lack of an alternative.

As summarised recently by Barry Eichengreen of Berkeley:

"The euro is a currency without a state. The renminbi is a currency with too much state. The SDR (special drawing rights at the IMF) is funny money. It is not, in fact, a currency".

The survival of the Euro and the fleshing out of its institutional framework in the period ahead fundamentally changes this position. Sparked by its existential crisis and just 13 years after its launch, the Euro is now firmly on the path to have the fiscal, banking and political underpinning to credibly rival the dollar. The long era of the 'exorbitant privilege' is drawing to a close.

By many measures, the Euro-zone economy has already over-taken that of the US. Its exports are nearly double its counterpart across the Atlantic. Its payments position with the rest of the world is in broad balance, compared to the persistent deficit of the US. Its fiscal deficit and public debt position is markedly more comfortable. Arguably most important of all, and in marked contrast to their US peers, its key policy-makers have maintained a crucial attachment to the role of their currency as a store of value.

This latter point in particular will resonate more and more strongly with private investors, central bank reserve managers and all of those looking for a stable unit of account in which to conduct trade or hold wealth. Their current disproportionate exposure to the dollar ultimately will be looked back upon as an historical aberration.

While it is impossible to predict the timing of such a development, it is certainly time for Euro-zone based investors to check their exposure to the dollar.

Simply put, if you have an investment portfolio or a pension fund, it is time to apply the much-quoted observation of Nietzsche to the recent travails of the Euro:

"What doesn't kill you makes you stronger".

32: TIME TO BE WARY OF THE QUEEN'S SHILLING

The Sunday Times, 13 January 2013

The massive increase in government debt of many developed countries has generated much commentary and concern in recent years. As talk of 'fiscal cliffs' and the multiple effects of prolonged 'austerity' fill the newsstands and airwaves, the tackling of government deficits and debt levels has dominated the policy agenda from Washington to Dublin and beyond.

The graph below, depicting the explosion in public debt as a percentage of GDP in the US, captures the experience of many countries whose debt levels have soared to multi-decade highs during this period of prolonged economic stagnation:

US Total Public Debt as a % of GDP

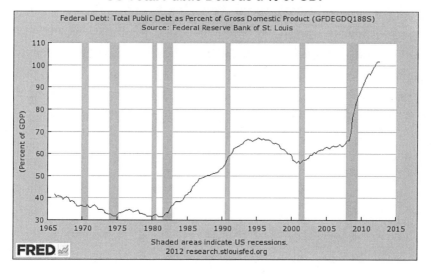

The debate about how these governments will move to ease this burden to a more 'sustainable' level has been loud and often contentious. In the context of the heavily indebted countries in the Euro-zone, some commentary has declared passionately in favour of default. More broadly, many have drawn the lessons of numerous historic examples and argued that a substantial acceleration in inflation will be the preferred, and indeed inevitable, mechanism to ease the heavy debt-loads.

I believe that a more likely path is currently being pursued with particular vigour, but little fanfare, across the Irish Sea: a path with significant implications for investors everywhere.

The next time you travel North or East and have cause to withdraw sterling from an ATM, take a moment to read the promise on the familiar note with the Queen's head. If it's a stg£20 note, the inscription will read:

"I promise to pay the bearer on demand the sum of 20 pounds".

In practice, you are free to take this note to the Bank of England whose staff will happily exchange it for two 10-pound notes, four five-pound notes, or even 20 one-pound notes if you so demand. This promise by the Bank to exchange 'paper' for 'paper' is clearly a very unusual type of asset (for you) / liability (for them). It is the power to make and have accepted this extraordinary promise, in payment for other assets, that is now being deployed to tackle the debt-load of Her Majesty's Government.

The Bank of England is now the proud owner of 25% of the outstanding debt of the UK government. It has created an irredeemable, zero interest rate obligation on itself in the form of many billions of pounds sterling, and used this extraordinary promise to purchase many billions of pounds of interest-bearing UK government debt:

Central Bank Ownership of Sovereign Debt

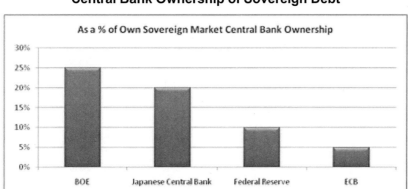

There is no need for a default. The threat of inflation is minimal in this era of abundant spare capacity. Instead, the government debt burden is being eased by a key arm of the State, the central bank, purchasing a large proportion of the government's debt with a 'paper' promise accruing no interest and with no maturity date.

There are two key implications of this for the investor:

- Be wary of storing your wealth in an asset (cash) that is being created in unprecedented amounts to ease unprecedented levels of government debt. It is preferable to own attractively valued real assets such as property or stocks that accrue a real income in rents and dividends;

- If you must have exposure to 'paper' promises, steer clear of that being made by our nearest neighbour: this is a time to be particularly wary of the Queen's shilling!

33: THE GEITHNER DOCTRINE FAVOURS STOCKS

The Sunday Times, 17 March 2013

Global stock markets have risen substantially in recent years. Stock investors have more than doubled their money since March 2009: €100 invested in the MSCI global index four years ago is worth over €201 today.

As the market has risen, the debate between those who believe that stocks are overvalued (usually relative to some historic metrics) and others who continue to see value (witness the recent purchase of Heinz by Warren Buffett) has grown more heated.

In contrast to a conventional attempt to pronounce on the outlook for economic growth, inflation or interest rates, or indeed to offer an analysis derived from balance sheets, income and cash-flow statements, I want to make a case for exposure to stocks based on an historic policy decision by a little-discussed US Treasury Secretary who has recently returned to the anonymity of private life.

There are numerous reasons why historians like to characterise significant policy positions as doctrines. In particular, the elevation of a policy to the status of a doctrine is often a signal of a change with major implications for the future.

Some examples may be helpful:

- The Monroe doctrine of 1823 saw newly re-elected US President Monroe warn that 'further efforts by European nations to colonize land or interfere with states in North or South America would be viewed as acts of aggression'. The end of European interference in the Western Hemisphere is directly traceable to this doctrine;

- Over a century later, the Truman doctrine of 1947 – justifying US involvement in the Greek civil war – set the scene for East/West confrontation around the globe for much of the next half-century;

- More recently the Bush doctrine following 9/11/2001 – asserting the right of the US to wage preventive war in self-defence – signalled a decade (and counting) of US military engagement in Afghanistan, Iraq and elsewhere.

I believe that the unheralded doctrine of outgoing US Treasury Secretary Timothy Geithner – formulated in the wake of the collapse of Lehman Brothers in 2008 – ultimately will hold as prominent a place in the history books as any of these well-known examples. More importantly, it continues to have significant implications for global monetary policy and stock-market investors.

The decision by Bush Treasury Secretary Paulson to allow a major bank to collapse sparked a massive contraction in global trade and activity. By many measures, the post-Lehman contraction was greater than that experienced at the onset of the great depression of the 1930s. Indeed, some argued reasonably that a greater cataclysm would likely follow. This lesson was not lost on Paulson's young successor.

The Geithner doctrine has never been formally stated in public. However, it is clear that a policy of protecting bank depositors and their legal equivalents – regardless of the losses of their banks – has been unbreakably in place since his appointment. The option of risking another Lehman-type collapse has been consistently eschewed. Moreover, this doctrine has been adopted as an all but universal one by policy-makers grappling with struggling banks around the globe.

The Geithner doctrine has underpinned the pay-outs by the Irish government to depositors and their legal equivalents in failed banks in Ireland. The Geithner doctrine has underpinned the UK government's pay-outs to British depositors and their legal equivalents in failed British and Icelandic banks. As recently as last month, the Geithner doctrine underpinned the Dutch government's pay-outs to depositors and their legal equivalents in the failed Dutch bank, SNS Reaal. The next few weeks also are likely to see the Geithner doctrine underpin pay-outs by the government in Cyprus to depositors and their legal equivalents in failed banks there.

The fundamental goal of the Geithner doctrine is the protection of the global financial and banking system. For policy-makers across the globe, concern about the moral hazard of what this means in practice has been trumped by the post-Lehman economic collapse.

As citizens and taxpayers we may take issue with this, but as investors we should draw the key conclusion – historically-low interest rates and massively-expanded central bank balance sheets are not temporary aberrations. They are the new and continuing normal. To protect the global financial and banking system, monetary policy is set to remain extraordinarily easy for many years to come. The Geithner doctrine demands it. The case for a meaningful exposure to stocks remains compelling.

US Official Short-Term Interest Rate

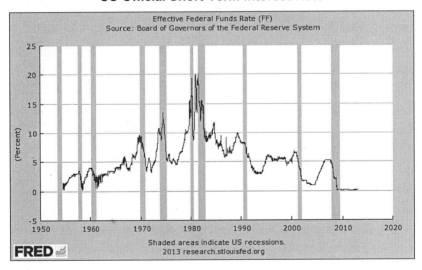

Assets of the US Central Bank

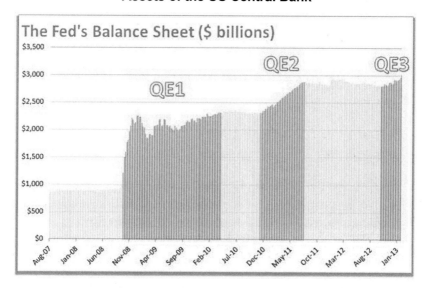

Source: The Federal Reserve Board of Governors.

34: IT IS SIMPLE: WHEN MONEY IS EASY COME, IT'S EVEN EASIER GO

The Sunday Times, 21 April 2013

"The process by which banks create money is so simple that the mind is repelled. When something so important is involved, a deeper mystery seems only decent." **J.K. Galbraith, 1975**

To the wry amusement of former Harvard Professor of Economics John Kenneth Galbraith, there is little mystery to money creation. Private banks create most of our money out of thin air. The small amount of paper printed or coin minted is all but irrelevant. Over 97% of the money circulating today in major economies like the US, Japan or the Euro-zone has been loaned into existence by private banks.

This money is invariably loaned to governments, households and corporations at interest rates higher than that paid on the deposits created. On the assumption that their debtors pay them back, private banks have a compelling incentive to loan into existence as much money as possible.

Since the collapse of Bretton Woods and the removal of any effective constraint on their capacity to issue loans, it is small wonder that there has been an explosion of money loaned into existence by private banks in recent decades. The evolution of debt to GDP for both the private and public sectors in the US, as depicted in the graph below, has been broadly replicated across the developed world:

US Debt to GDP: Private and Public

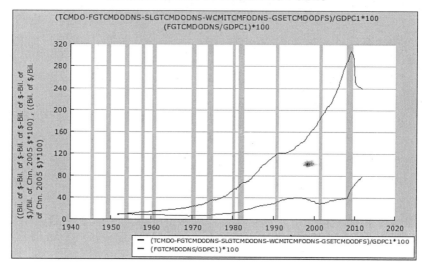

In conjunction with this explosion of money loaned into existence, the riskiness of those issuing the loans also has increased greatly. Speaking in the wake of the global financial crisis, this was summarised clearly in a major speech in New York in 2010 by Bank of England Governor Mervyn King:

> "While banks' balance sheets have exploded, so have the risks associated with those balance sheets. Capital ratios have declined and leverage has risen. Immediately prior to the crisis, leverage in the banking system of the industrialised world had increased to astronomical levels. Simple leverage ratios of close to 50% or more could be found in the US, UK, and the continent of Europe".

The dramatic results of any disruption to this explosion in money and risk are now well known. As put characteristically well in 2010 by the author and trader, Nassim Taleb:

> "The banking system seems to have lost more on risk-taking than every penny *ever* earned taking risks. The same happened in 1983 with banks losing cumulatively every penny ever made, and in 1991-1992 when the Savings and Loans industry became history".

In summary, risky private banks create almost all of our money and they have a compelling incentive to create as much money as possible and no effective constraint on doing so. However, as we have seen since the initial tremor from the sub-prime mortgage market in the US in 2007, any disruption to this shaky system can cause widespread market and economic turmoil.

Such disruptions are inevitable. Market and economic turmoil stemming from the money creation of private banks are certain but impossible to predict. As Taleb famously observed, they are 'known unknowns': we know that they will happen, but we have no way of knowing when.

For investors, this is the fundamental case for portfolio diversification. A diversified portfolio is both less exposed to, and more equipped to take advantage of, these inevitable periods of turmoil.

I think the following thought experiment from Ted Lucas of Lattice Strategies in 2011 captures the message well:

"Imagine a portfolio that was down 20% during the 2008 implosion *versus* a portfolio that was down 40%. In the 2009 rebound, assume the first portfolio recovered by 25%, while the second rebounded by 40%. At the end of the two periods, the first portfolio would be back to its starting point, while the second – after knocking the lights out in 2009 – would still be down 16%, requiring another 19% gain to get back to even (i.e., a 40% gain on 60 cents on the dollar yields 84 cents; to get 84 cents back to a full dollar requires a further 19% gain)".

35: SOVIET EXPERIENCE SHOULD BE RED FLAG SIGNAL TO CENTRAL PLANNERS

The Sunday Times, 2 June 2013

The extraordinarily easy stance of global monetary policy continues to dominate financial markets. The negative shocks of recent months, such as the budget sequestration in the US, the post-election uncertainty in Italy, or the unprecedented depositor haircut in Cyprus, have all been trumped by the continued commitment of global central banks to cheap and easy money.

The Federal Reserve remains wedded to practically zero interest rates and ongoing quantitative easing (QE). The European Central Bank (ECB) has cut interest rates to an historic low and continues to provide the backstop of its Outright Monetary Transactions programme (OMT). The incoming Governor of the Bank of England (BoE) is openly searching for new levers to ease policy. The Bank of Japan (BoJ) has announced a new range of 'quantitative and qualitative monetary easing' measures under newly appointed Governor Kuroda.

Unsurprisingly, the demand for global 'risk' assets such as stocks and corporate debt shows no sign of abating. Stock investors, in particular, are benefitting greatly, while savers are suffering from ever-lower deposit rates.

I believe it's time investors thought a little deeper about such centrally-planned dominance.

Following the collapse of the Soviet Union, it quickly became commonplace to view its demise as inevitable. In particular, many viewed an economic system where the allocation of resources was determined by the input-output equations of government bureaucrats, and not the price signals generated by the demand and supply of market forces, as ultimately doomed to failure. So it seemed proved across Central and Eastern Europe in the dramatic days of 1989 and 1990.

A good example of how market forces *via* a price signal prompt, or some might say force, decisions was the emergence of the so-called 'bond market vigilantes' in the US Treasury market in the first term of the Clinton Presidency. Investors, unhappy about a rising budget deficit and government debt levels, shunned the Treasury market forcing bond yields (interest rates) higher. The power of this signal was captured in this much-quoted quip from Clinton adviser, James Carville, at the time:

> "I used to think if there was reincarnation, I wanted to come back as the President or the Pope or a .400 baseball hitter. But now I want to come back as the bond market. You can intimidate everybody".

The signal proved effective. Clinton reined in the deficit and ultimately left a legacy of broad budget balance to his successor from Texas. Market forces had done their job.

Almost two decades later, a radical change has been imposed. In grappling for an effective response to their anaemic economies, monetary policy-makers effectively have taken control of their respective government bond markets.

Bond yields in these economies are now what the bureaucrats at the Federal Reserve, the BoE, the ECB and the BoJ determine them to be.

Extraordinarily, with annual inflation of up to 3% in most of these countries, nominal government bond yields out to 30 years are now well below this level.

The market forces of demand and supply are no longer the generator of these key price signals. The 'bond market vigilantes' so revered and feared by Carville have been put to the sword.

The full consequences of this radical intervention are impossible to predict. However, there seems little reason to believe that this modern attempt at central planning ultimately will prove any more successful than its Soviet predecessor. History suggests we should be wary and not complacent of centrally-planned dominance.

Beyond wariness, investors should be paying particular attention to the advice of Howard Marks in his book, *The Most Important Thing: Uncommon Sense for the Thoughtful Investor*. He mused that if he offered to sell somebody his car, that somebody would ask the price before saying "Yes" or "No".

"Deciding on an investment without carefully considering the fairness of its price is just as silly", he writes. "But when people decide, without disciplined consideration, to own something, as they did with tech stocks in the late 1990s – or that they won't own something, as they did with junk bonds in the 1970s and early 1980s – that's just what they're doing. Bottom line: there is no such thing as a good or bad idea regardless of price".

36: WHY VALUE INVESTING WON'T FALL FLAT

The Sunday Times, 21 July 2013

Forbes magazine has been publishing its famous list of America's richest people, the Forbes 400, since 1982. While there have been many entries and exits over the last 31 years, the position of Warren Buffett at or near the top of the list and its global equivalent, the Forbes World's Billionaires List, has been an enduring constant.

The investor from Omaha, Nebraska has translated his value investing philosophy into the consistently largest fortune on the planet.

Modern finance theory argues that the success of Buffett is unskilled luck and should be ignored, since it is impossible to 'beat' the market and those like Buffett who have done so are merely the lucky beneficiaries of a random outcome.

The Efficient Markets Hypothesis at the heart of this theory was passionately summarised in a debate some years ago by its originator Eugene Fama of the University of Chicago, when he proclaimed: "God knows markets are efficient". In many lecture halls and trading rooms over the last four decades, to argue otherwise has been to flirt with heresy.

If Buffett were the sole success of value investing it would be impossible to disagree with Fama and the conclusion of modern finance theory that market prices are the efficient discounters of all known information and that attempting to 'beat' the market is the pointless pursuit of the stubbornly deluded. However, there is a substantial body of evidence to suggest that value investing has been consistently successful in 'beating' the market.

Most convincingly for me is the article written by Buffett and published in the Columbia Business School magazine in the autumn of 1984: 'The Super-Investors of Graham and Doddsville'. In disarmingly simple language, Buffett makes a compelling case for the value investing approach first formalised by Ben Graham and David Dodd over 70 years ago. By defining 'a common intellectual home' for a group of stunningly successful investors as the mythical 'Graham and Doddsville', Buffett shows how their success cannot be the result of unskilled luck and is overwhelmingly likely to be the result of their shared but variously applied value investing philosophy.

The results in the table below are of the 'Super-Investors' referred to in the article – a highly recommended and enjoyable read for anyone with an interest in investing:

Fund	Manager	Fund Period	Fund Return	Market Return p.a.
WJS Limited	Walter J. Schloss	1956-1984	21.3%	8.4%
TEK Limited	Tom Knapp	1968-1983	20.0%	7.0%
Buffett Partnership	Warren Buffett	1957-1969	29.5%	7.4%
Sequoia Fund	William J. Ruane	1970-1984	18.2%	10.0%
Charles Munger Limited	Charles Munger	1962-1975	19.8%	5.0%
Pacific Partners Limited	Rick Guerin	1965-1983	32.9%	7.8%
Perlmeter Investments	Stan Perlmeter	1965-1983	23.0%	7.0%
Washington Post Trust	3 different managers	1978-1983	21.8%	7.0%
FMC Pension Fund	8 different managers	1975-1983	17.1%	12.6%

The central tenet of value investing is that every asset has an intrinsic value. In the words of Buffett to the shareholders of his company Berkshire Hathaway in 1999:

"Intrinsic value can be defined simply: it is the discounted value of the cash that can be taken out of a business during its remaining life. As our definition suggests, intrinsic value is an estimate rather than a precise figure and two people looking at the same set of facts will almost inevitably come up with different intrinsic value figures".

Before investing in an asset, the challenge is to apply the approach of Graham and Dodd – built on since by their followers such as Buffett – to estimating its intrinsic value. Only then can a decision be made as to whether this value is sufficiently attractive relative to its market price to warrant an investment. While different value investors often will arrive at different decisions by using different techniques or will differ on the emphasis they accord the various inputs to their valuations, they are united in their goal to seek and exploit this difference between value and price.

At a value investing course in Columbia some years ago, Bruce Greenwald, the renowned academic successor to Ben Graham, told two of my colleagues that, despite its success, he believed that less than 5% of investors follow a value philosophy. This would be no surprise to Buffett who ended his 1984 article by making a rare prediction:

"Ships will sail around the world but the Flat Earth Society will flourish. There will continue to be wide discrepancies between price and value in the marketplace, and those who read their Graham & Dodd will continue to prosper".

It might be worth pondering whether you or the funds you invest in are free of the investment equivalent of what the most successful investor of all time calls 'Flat Earth' thinking.

37: WHAT THE PREMIER LEAGUE TEACHES INVESTORS

The Irish Times, 3 September 2013

The annual circus of the Premier League has rolled into town again. Whether you are a devoted fan or an involuntary bystander to the thrills and dramas of the next nine months, the wall-to-wall coverage of the self-styled best league in the world will make it difficult to ignore.

If you can briefly forget about the football however, there is one feature of the Premier League this year that highlights an important lesson for investors looking to select a fund manager: the retirement of Alex Ferguson as manager of Manchester United, and more particularly, the incredible league record he leaves behind after 27 seasons in charge at Old Trafford.

Relative to the likes of Liverpool, Everton, Leeds or Arsenal, who had all captured the league title on numerous occasions since United had last triumphed, there was no reason to expect any particular success when Ferguson arrived from Aberdeen.

Indeed, if the previous 18 league campaigns were anything to go by, the faithful of the Stretford End were facing another long period of failure and disappointment.

The Ferguson record defied this outlook. He achieved unprecedented success while Liverpool, Everton, Leeds and Arsenal sacked and hired multiple managers to little effect.

While Ferguson may have had exceptional managerial skill, it is unlikely that the 41 managers who passed through the revolving doors at Anfield, Goodison Park, Elland Road and Highbury during the long years of his remarkable dominance were as unskilled as their performance records suggest.

The more likely explanation is that some or possibly many of them possessed the skill to perform better, but few if any of them were given the time.

This is the crucially important lesson for those assessing the similarly volatile world of investing. Over the shorter-term, market 'mood' and those lucky enough to be exposed to it may perform but over the longer term the effects of 'mood' fades and the skilful manager, if still around, is more likely to prevail.

The graph below shows how market 'mood' has dominated stock-market performance in any given year, while over any given five years, performance has been dominated by factors rooted in the health of the underlying businesses: dividend yield and dividend growth:

Market 'Mood' Fades over Time

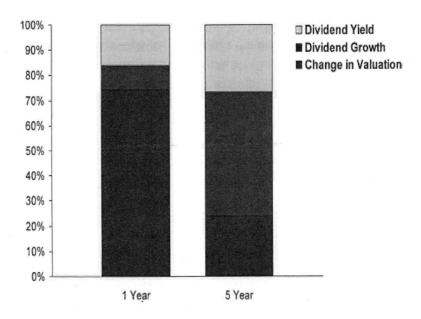

S&P500, 1871-2010 – *Source*: GMO

These factors are more likely to be identified by the skilful than the lucky, but crucially skill needs time to come to the fore. Long-term success in football or investing is most likely achieved by a manager with a credible process who is given the time to apply it.

The author Nassim Taleb summarized it well in his book, *Fooled by Randomness: The Hidden Role of Chance in Life and in the Markets*:

> "Over a short time increment, one observes the variability of a portfolio, not the returns. When I see an investor monitoring his portfolio with live prices on his cellular telephone or his handheld, I smile and smile".

Paradoxically, investors in general have been rushing in the opposite direction. Reacting to more and more 'news' from a rapidly-expanding media, they have been shortening their time-frame. Whether hiring and firing managers or buying and selling assets, the average investor has increasingly eschewed the longer view.

A good proxy illustration of this is the average holding period for stocks. The trend on the NYSE, where the average holding period for stocks is now just six months compared to over six years in the late 1970s, is true of stock-markets everywhere:

Average Holding Period for Stocks on NYSE

Source: NYSE

When investing you should stay clear of such frenzied behaviour. Better to devote your time and energy to finding a manager whose approach is credible and understandable. You should check then to ensure that they have demonstrated the courage to consistently apply this approach through the inevitable vagaries of the marketplace. Finally, you should relax and allow time to deliver your likely performance reward.

The advice of renowned Canadian investor Peter Cundhill in the 10th anniversary letter to the fortunate investors in his Cundhill Value Fund in 1984 is worth repeating and repeating:

> "The most important attribute for success in investing is patience, patience, and more patience; the majority of investors do not possess this characteristic".

He could equally have been referring to football fans or club chairmen. Enjoy the season.

38: DON'T FORGET THE LESSONS OF LTCM

The Irish Times, 16 September 2013

This is a month of anniversaries. Five years ago this month, Lehman Brothers collapsed dramatically. The global credit system froze and, as trust between banks, and between banks and their customers, was shaken violently, global trade and activity descended in a frightening downward spiral. Indeed, the descent of the global economy accelerated to a pace not seen since the great depression. The most challenging half-decade for economic policy since Roosevelt entered the White House had begun. We are still grappling with the consequences.

While the collapse of the New York investment bank and its aftermath contains many lessons for investors and policy-makers, the anniversary that I want to comment on is from 10 years earlier: the September 1998 collapse of the hedge fund Long Term Capital Management (LTCM).

Although the impact of the collapse of LTCM was short-lived and minor relative to that of Lehman, judging from many client meetings to this day, I believe it contains a crucial lesson for investors that needs recalling.

LTCM was a hedge fund started with great expectations in 1994. By combining the academic credentials of Robert Merton and Myron Scholes with the legendary Wall Street skills of John Meriwether and his ex-Salomon team – Michael Lewis's book, *Liar's Poker*, gives a wonderful account of their Salomon days – LTCM set out to transform its quantitative mastery of risk into a spectacularly successful money-machine.

The central assumption of the LTCM investment strategy was that the historic volatility of securities prices was a sufficient proxy for future volatility and therefore a credible proxy measurement of risk.

Armed with this ability to model and measure risk, LTCM could profit from exploiting situations where market prices differed from their model prices. Secure in their belief that such market mispricing would be ironed out in time, they could then lever their exposure to these situations to a massive degree and accrue the massive rewards.

Following three years of annualised returns touching 40% and the awarding of the 1997 Nobel Prize in Economics to Merton and Scholes, the strategy and central assumption of LTCM seemed convincingly vindicated. A happy and rewarding future beckoned for the Connecticut-based money-machine and its lucky clients.

Nine months after the triumph of the Nobel Prize in Stockholm, LTCM imploded. Its clients were wiped out and the reverberations of its collapse were felt globally. While its extensive use of leverage clearly played a role, it's also clear that the strategy and the central assumption on which it was based had crumbled in the face of the August 1998 Russian debt default.

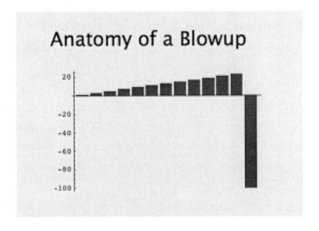

Source: Nassim Taleb, 'The Fourth Quadrant: A Map of the Limits of Statistics'

The metaphor of the turkey and its life-cycle in the run-up to Christmas day, as recounted by Nassim Taleb in his essay, 'The Fourth Quadrant: A Map of the Limits of Statistics', gives us a crucial insight into this dramatic collapse:

> "My classical metaphor: A turkey is fed for 1,000 days – every day confirms to its statistical department that the human race cares

about its welfare 'with increased statistical significance'. On the 1,001st day (Christmas Day), the turkey has a surprise".

If the fate of the turkey doesn't concern you, consider this quote from *Titanic* Captain E.J. Smith on the eve of its only voyage:

"When anyone asks me how I can best describe my experience in nearly 40 years at sea, I merely say, uneventful. Of course there have been winter gales, and storms and fog and the like. But in all my experience, I have never been in any accident of any sort worth speaking about. I have seen but one vessel in distress in all my years at sea. I never saw a wreck and never have been wrecked nor was I ever in any predicament that threatened to end in disaster of any sort".

The story of the turkey in the run-up to Christmas day and the Titanic Captain in the run-up to launch is analogous to that of LTCM in the run-up to the Russian default.

In this month of anniversaries, the lesson from 15 years ago – that the only thing measured by historic volatility is historic volatility – needs recalling. Investors, regulators, banks and their risk-managers who continue to use it as a measure of risk are destined to suffer the fate of the turkey and Captain Smith. Try not to be among them.

39: ALLOCATING FUND ASSETS IS STILL A TRICKY BALANCING ACT

The Irish Times, 1 October 2013

The balanced fund diversified across a range of asset classes has been a staple choice of long-term savers for decades.

Seeking to harvest the benefits of diversification and provide an attractive long-term return, balanced funds are likely to remain a popular choice for many individuals and institutions looking for a long-term home for their savings.

In Ireland, the so-called 'managed fund' offered by a range of domestic and international investment managers has traditionally fulfilled this role. Notwithstanding the growing range of investment funds now on offer here, the managed fund is likely to continue to fulfil this role for many years to come.

While there has been some tendency to broaden the asset classes invested in by managed funds, equities and sovereign bonds generally represent between 80% and 90% of the average fund. The key asset allocation decision is therefore that between equities and sovereign bonds. This is the crucial asset allocation challenge facing the managed fund manager.

Ben Graham, the man widely acknowledged as the father of value investing, summarised his deceptively simple approach to this challenge over 80 years ago:

"A fundamental guiding rule is that the investor should never have less than 25% or more than 75% in common stocks, with a consequent inverse range of between 75% and 25% in bonds. There is an implication here that the standard division should be an equal one, or 50-50 between the two major investment mediums.

> However, the only (investment) principle that has ever worked well consistently is to buy common stocks at such times as they are cheap by analysis, and to sell them at such times as they are dear by analysis. That sounds like timing; but it is not really timing at all but rather the purchase and sale of securities by the method of valuation".

The extraordinary monetary policy response to the global financial and economic crisis of recent years continues to have a major impact on the valuation of asset classes.

The valuation of cash and bonds relative to equities and to their longer-term history looks unattractive, while the valuation of equities relative to cash and bonds looks correspondingly attractive, but considerably less so when compared to its longer-term history.

For Graham, this would likely suggest an asset allocation at or near the upper end of his maximum exposure to equities of 75%.

However, before the modern managed fund manager hastens to replicate this allocation, some thought as to the differences in context from the time of Graham is warranted.

In particular, the markedly different monetary regime and the markedly more active policy environment have introduced uncertainties that were never faced by the father of value investing.

It may be little wonder that one of his most famous successors, Seth Klarman of Baupost, recently decided to return money to his investors, opining in the process:

> "Investing today may well be harder than it has been at any time in our three decades of existence, not because markets are falling but because they are rising; not because governments have failed to act but because they chronically overreact; not because we lack acumen or analytical tools, but because the range of possible outcomes remains enormously wide; and not because there are no opportunities, but because the underpinnings of our economy and financial system are so precarious that the unabating risks of collapse dwarf all other factors".

Valuation must remain central to the equity *versus* bond decision. But even with this insight from Ben Graham, the challenge of asset allocation for the managed fund manager has arguably never been as difficult.

If you have invested in a managed fund, or your pension scheme has invested in one, it might be worth asking the manager how he or she is addressing this challenge.

40: JOIN THE STOCK MARKET RALLY BUT STEER CLEAR OF THOSE HERDS

The Sunday Times, 27 October 2013

Investor demand for stocks shows little sign of abating. The continued rise of global stock markets has seen them gain over 130% since March 2009, to sit today just 3.5% below their all-time high of October 2007.

Potential negative factors in recent months, such as the threatened escalation of the conflict in Syria, the increasing debate about the timing and extent of Fed 'tapering', and the budget stalemate and government shut-down in the US, have all failed to deter the flow of investor money into stocks.

Amid the excitement of rising prices, it is important to remember that following the sharp rally of recent years, the absolute valuation of stocks is by definition less attractive. The value generally on offer in stock markets today cannot be as enticing as it has been over the last four and a half years.

However, with short-rates, sovereign and corporate yields all remaining markedly lower than 'normal', the relative valuation of stocks to such competing assets is continuing to attract investor demand.

The graph below from UBS in January is still a good summary snapshot of this situation:

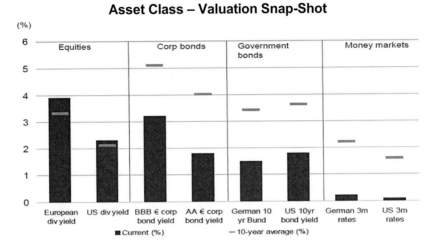

Source: UBS. As at 24 January 2013

This may well continue. Never forget, however, that predicting the future direction of the *general* stock-market is notoriously challenging. There are just too many variables.

Indeed, it is arguable that the range of variables confronting the investor today makes the task more challenging than ever.

Investing in a portfolio of individually-analysed, sensibly-diversified and conservatively-valued companies is likely to prove a more rewarding decision.

For those looking to participate in the stock market rally therefore, or thinking of entrusting some of their low-yielding savings to a professional manager, the following general, sensible rules should be kept in mind:

- **Try to be conservative**: Before, during and after every investment, try to keep asking the question: what can go wrong? You won't always avoid trouble, but across a portfolio over time it's likely to increase your chance of success;

- **Try to be contrarian**: The herd mentality of human beings, and especially those in financial markets, is well documented. An independent mindset is likely to prove a more rewarding approach;

- **Try to be flexible**: There is no magic number or set of metrics that guarantees investment success. If there was, it would have been discovered and exploited years ago. In searching for value, it is important to be flexible in where you look;

- **Try to be long-term**: In this era of exploding media and plummeting transaction costs, the frenzy of short-term trading continues to intensify. Most of this is the pointless chasing of noise. By taking a longer perspective and trying to avoid the noise, a better investment return is likely.

41: WHY IT'S TIME TO CRY "MAMA"

The Sunday Business Post, 24 November 2013

The regular procession of bank management, followed by their central bank peers, parading in front of a baying Dáil Finance committee has become repetitive. The banks have little incentive to tackle the crisis in mortgage arrears. The central bank has little power to change this. The politicians seem content to have a populist stage on which to compete in pointless emoting. Yet over 60% of Irish mortgages in arrears are owed to Irish taxpayer-owned banks: AIB, PTSB and IBRC. It is time to break the log-jam.

After the collapse of Irish property prices and the resulting collapse of confidence in the value of the property-related loan assets of the Irish banks, the government intervened to try to restore confidence in the banking system by setting up the National Asset Management Agency (NAMA). The lengthy debate about the rights, the wrongs or the arguable mistakes in design of this intervention does not concern me here. My focus is on the key features of the NAMA framework, which with a minor modification can substantially break the mortgage arrears log-jam. Let's call that mechanism the Mortgage Asset Management Agency: MAMA.

The NAMA framework created a new institution, NAMA, which transferred a new asset, NAMA bonds, to the Irish banks in return for an asset in which confidence had collapsed: the property-related loan assets of the Irish banks.

The two key features of relevance in this framework are:

- The risk to the future value of the property-related loan assets is borne by NAMA;

- The European Central Bank (ECB) accepts NAMA bonds as collateral to secure funding at the ECB refinancing rate – currently 0.25%.

The balance sheet of NAMA is thus:

NAMA - Balance Sheet

Assets	Liabilities
Property-related loan assets	NAMA bonds

In equivalent fashion, the MAMA framework would create a new institution, MAMA, which would transfer a new asset, MAMA bonds, to the Irish banks (note: in order to avoid any further subsidy of the banking system by the beleaguered taxpayer, the only banks included in this process would be those currently owned by the taxpayer: AIB, PTSB and IBRC) in return for that portion of their mortgage assets that are currently in arrears. The modification in comparison to NAMA is that these mortgage assets would be transferred to MAMA at par.

The two key features of relevance in this framework would then be:

- The risk to the future value of the mortgage assets would be borne by MAMA;

- The ECB would accept MAMA bonds as collateral to secure funding at the ECB refinancing rate – currently 0.25%.

The balance sheet of MAMA would thus be:

MAMA - Balance Sheet

Assets	Liabilities
Mortgage Assets	MAMA bonds

Distressed Irish mortgage holders in Irish taxpayer-owned banks would then have a single, standardised entity with which to engage. It would be an entity, like NAMA, with an explicit mandate to recoup as much as possible for the taxpayer, while working sensibly with its debtor clients.

Clearly, as with NAMA, those debtors who failed to act in good faith would suffer accordingly. However, those prepared to act in good faith would have a realistic opportunity to work their way through to a sustainable solution. The recently reported success of developers Michael O'Flynn and Sean Mulryan, in emerging soon from NAMA in a solvent and sustainable position, shows how an equivalent process could succeed for future debtors of MAMA.

Indeed, by building on the experience of NAMA, MAMA should be particularly well positioned to fulfil its mandate in a sensitive, thorough and credible fashion. There is no need to re-invent the institutional and operational wheel. We are fortunate to have the template. More than that, we are fortunate to have a live equivalent with over four years of operation under its belt.

The sharp increase in the market value of the taxpayer-owned Irish banks following such an intervention also should be highlighted. The market herd that now values banks across the globe at a much higher level than heretofore is running in our favour. Examples such as the recent advance in the Bank of Ireland share price or the recent sale by the UK government of some of its shareholding in Lloyds are particularly encouraging. Some, if not all, of the cost of MAMA would be offset by this benign revaluation.

There are many details missing from such a broadly-outlined proposal. For example, the absence of the non-taxpayer-owned banks would need to be considered separately, but should not be a reason for delay in tackling over 60% of the problem now. More challengingly, the agreement of the ECB would be crucial and is unlikely to be straight-forward. That said, having regularly modified our bail-out programme, financed NAMA, and 'noted' the redemption of the Anglo promissory notes, the ECB has shown an encouraging willingness to respond positively to imaginative suggestions to tackle the legacy of our boom and bust.

We must now make the case that the crisis in mortgage arrears is clearly part of this painful legacy. A fair and sustainable solution for distressed mortgage debtors and the Irish taxpayer must be found. We have NAMA for the big boys. We need a NAMA for everybody else. We need a MAMA.

42: IRISH BONDS BOUNCED BACK SO FAR, I'M OFF TO PORTUGAL

The Sunday Times, 2 March 2014

There has never been a less rewarding time to buy or own Irish government bonds. The collapse in the borrowing costs of the Irish government, accelerated by a successful bail-out exit and the credit upgrade by Moody's, has been remarkable. Irish bond yields are now touching historic lows. It is time to sell.

From an annual interest rate of almost 14% in July 2011, the Irish government can now borrow money on a 10-year basis at an annual rate of just over 3% - see the graph below. The few who believed that the Irish government would pay its debts in full and on time has clearly turned into the many.

Irish Government 10-Year Bond Yield

Source: Bloomberg.

The prescient few have enjoyed a correspondingly remarkable return. For example, an investment of €100 in the Irish government 10-year bond in the summer of 2011 is worth well over €200 today. Indeed, buying any Irish government bond at any time over the past few years has yielded a handsome profit.

The economist Colm McCarthy has suggested that the Irish economic experience of recent years warrants two chapters in the textbooks of the future: the first for one of the most incredible economic booms in history; the second for one of the most incredible economic busts. I think a third separate chapter is also warranted: to cover the incredible journey of the Irish government bond market.

I am almost certain that the Irish government will pay its debt in full and on time. When the risk of this view being wrong is offset by an attractive interest rate, a strong case can be made for buying or holding Irish government bonds. However, when that compensation has been reduced to the point of extinction, the case for buying or holding the bonds also disappears. This has now happened in Ireland.

If you want a better-value proposition in Euro-zone government bonds, the annual rate on offer on the Portuguese government 10-year of almost 5% is worth considering. I believe that the Portuguese government, no less than its Irish counterpart, also will pay its debt in full and on time. However, in contrast with Ireland, I feel investors are still compensated for any lingering doubts on this issue. A 5% annual return in the current low interest rate environment should certainly be on the radar.

Elsewhere, predicting the direction of the general stock market is notoriously challenging. There are just too many variables. It is also important to remember that the absolute valuation of stocks is less attractive following the sharp rally of recent years. Yet investing in a portfolio of individually-analysed, sensibly-diversified, and conservatively-valued companies is likely to prove more rewarding than loaning your hard-earned savings to the Irish government at current yield levels.

The National Treasury Management Agency (NTMA) is credited by many as having navigated the choppy waters of international debt markets with considerable skill in recent years. As an investor, you should have no interest in loaning the NTMA anything at the return now on offer. As a citizen and tax-payer, however, you should implore it to borrow as much as possible for as long as possible at the current historically-low borrowing costs.

Sensibly invested in our capital and other needs, such borrowing could surely generate a return above this historically-cheap cost.

It is time for investors to sell Irish bonds but, more importantly, it is time the NTMA took to the same task with ambition and determination. There may never be a better opportunity.

43: GETTING ACTIVE THE BUFFETT WAY CAN BRING YOU GREAT REWARDS

The Sunday Times, 6 April 2014

Interest rates are at extraordinarily low levels and likely to remain there (see chart). Consequently, savers are challenged as seldom before to seek better returns than those offered by the traditional choice of bank deposits. The challenge was summarised ruefully by a property investor at a recent mass property auction in Dublin:

> "People are fed up having money and getting 1.25% from the bank. They're trying to maintain their pensions. That's why they're here".

I want to focus on how savers and investors should choose an investment approach likely to deliver a better reward than the meagre one on offer from bank deposits. There are only two broad approaches: passive and active investing.

In his recent letter to Berkshire Hathaway shareholders, Warren Buffett, the most successful active investor of all time, ironically made a strong case for the passive approach. Disclosing a snippet from his will on how his cash will be invested after death, he said:

> "My advice to the trustee could not be simpler. Put 10% of the cash in short-term government bonds and 90% in a very low-cost S&P 500 index fund. I believe the trust's long-term results from this policy will be superior to those attained by most investors, whether pension funds, institutions or individuals".

Buffett recommends this passive approach not because he believes that financial markets can't be beaten — his life is based on the conviction they can — but because he knows that few investors possess the skill to beat them.

While unarguably right about this, the case for active investing is nonetheless compelling. Indeed, the stunning track record of Buffett and many who have followed him goes a long way to supporting the active approach. Most convincing for me is *The Super-investors of Graham and Doddsville*, his article published in the Columbia Business School magazine in the autumn of 1984. In disarmingly simple language, Buffett makes a powerful case for the active value investing approach, formalized by Ben Graham and David Dodd more than 70 years ago. Buffett shows how their success cannot be the result of luck but is overwhelmingly likely to have resulted from their shared but variously applied philosophy of active value-investing.

For a host of systemic and behavioural reasons, financial markets are prone to lurch from euphoria to depression, and back again. The active investor is therefore regularly afforded the opportunity to take advantage of the inability of markets to value assets sensibly. We need look no further than the dramatic gyrations of Irish government bonds, property and stock markets over the past decade. The fact that few investors possess the skill to take advantage of this opportunity does not detract from the rewards that are on offer to those who do. As Buffett and others have shown, these rewards can be considerable.

Savers and investors looking to choose a market-beating active manager should concentrate on the following questions:

- Is the investment philosophy sensible and credible?
- Does the investment process flow sensibly and credibly from the philosophy?
- Are the people making the investment decisions capable of and incentivised to implement the process faithfully?
- Is the historical investment performance consistent with the philosophy and the process?

The future return offered by financial markets is always uncertain. However, the extraordinarily low return on offer from bank deposits is increasingly challenging savers and investors to embrace this uncertainty. In doing so, their first challenge is to decide between a passive and an active approach. Buffett may have recommended the former for after his death, but the latter can offer a markedly greater return.

In the case of the living Buffett and many who have followed his active value approach, the rewards achieved have been spectacularly greater. By choosing the rare manager with the right answers to a short list of the right questions, I believe there is a real chance for savers and investors to share in them.

ECB Policy Rate – 15 Year Chart

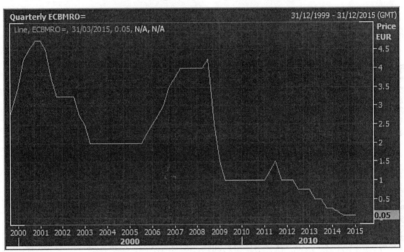

44: THE STING IN THE TAIL OF RISING HOUSE PRICES IS THE FALL IN THE VALUE OF MONEY

The Sunday Times, 11 May 2014

The enticing property supplements are back with gusto. The stock market is abuzz with the listing of no fewer than three real estate investment trusts (Reits) in recent months. With a combined firepower of almost €1nn to invest in Irish commercial and residential property, these Reits are joining many international and domestic investors in a quickening hunt for Irish property. The demand for Irish property and property-related assets is so strong that, contrary to the fears of many, the prospect of the National Asset Management Agency being profitably wound up years ahead of schedule is growing by the week.

My brother-in-law is a mortgage broker in Leixlip, Co Kildare – good morning, Leo! I asked him recently about his business and he answered that, not only has he seen a sharp pick-up in volume over the past nine to 12 months, there has also been a significant rise in prices.

He cited the example of a client who bought a three-bedroomed semi-detached house in Leixlip just over a year ago for €160,000 and noted that an equivalent house in the same estate sold recently for €222,000.

The airwaves and op-ed columns are full of opinions on what is driving this turn-around and what, if anything, citizens, investors and policy-makers should be doing about it. It is not my intention to add to the cacophony of voices debating the demand *versus* supply position in the Irish property market, but I do believe looking at the issue from a different perspective may be of benefit.

Charlie Munger is the long-time business partner of Warren Buffett and is also a spectacularly successful investor in his own right. Like Buffett, Munger likes to share his wisdom in thoughtful and digestible speeches. A particularly insightful nugget from a speech he made in 1986 throws some interesting light on the current behaviour of the Irish property market. Referring to the famous algebraist Jacobi, Munger said:

> "It is in the nature of things, as Jacobi knew, that many hard problems are best solved only when they are addressed backwards. Invert, always invert".

It is an interesting exercise to take this advice from Munger and to apply it to the example from Leo in Leixlip. The three-bedroomed semi-detached house has increased in price from €160,000 to €222,000 in just over a year, but it is also important to note the inverse – that a three-bedroomed semi-detached house could buy €160,000 just over a year ago, while an equivalent house today buys €222,000 or more.

Instead of just seeing the past year as a straightforward story of rising house prices, we should also see it as a story of falling money value. The same house in Leixlip can buy €62,000 more today than a year ago.

The process of money getting cheaper is also evident in other asset markets. For example, to buy 100 shares in an exchange traded fund (ETF) tracking the S&P 500 Index of US stocks cost €11,456 a year ago. Today it costs €13,479. In Munger terms, 100 shares in the S&P tracker bought €11,456 a year ago, while today those 100 shares buy €13,479.

This fall in money value is clearly not happening in a policy vacuum. Short-term interest rates in the US, the UK, Japan and the Eurozone have been at practically zero for a long time and look likely to stay there for a long time to come.

More controversially, these major central banks effectively have taken control of their government bond markets. The most glaring example is the UK, where the Bank of England is now the proud owner of 25% of the outstanding stock of UK gilts (see the graph below).

Navigating the path back to monetary policy normality is likely to be the key challenge for policy-makers and asset markets in the years ahead.

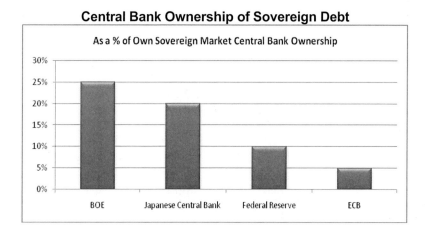

I have no view on the next move in Irish property prices. However, before embracing the delights of the freshly enticing property supplements, I think it is helpful to consider Munger and the insight he took from Jacobi, while also pondering the continuing, extraordinary monetary policy environment.

45: WHAT ARE YOU MOST WORRIED ABOUT?

The Sunday Times, 8 June 2014

I was delighted to present some thoughts on investing to a recent meeting of the Irish chapter of PRMIA, the Professional Risk Managers International Association.

In the lively questions and answers session that followed, one question was particularly striking:

> "As an investor facing into the uncertain future, what are you most worried about today?".

With stock markets scaling new highs, interest rates and bond yields tethered to new lows and positive property chatter growing louder by the week, it seems timely to consider some possible answers.

Geopolitical tensions are a perennial worry for investors. The oil crises of the 1970s, the first Gulf War of the early 1990s and the tragic felling of the Twin Towers on 9/11/2001 are just a few examples from recent decades where geopolitical pressures spilled over into financial market disruption. On a longer timeframe, there have been many others.

The current conflicts in Syria and the Ukraine, the rising tensions between China and Japan and the simmering discontent across much of the Islamic world are all potential flashpoints. More generally, the growing popular restlessness from Brazil to Turkey and South Africa to Egypt show a world struggling for stability in the face of multiple challenges.

While the dangers faced are serious and the danger of complacency is real, as an investor I am not particularly worried by the geopolitical tensions of today. Of course I could be wrong, but I believe the overwhelming incentives of the big four global powers of the US, China, the EU and Russia to maintain a broadly stable global system will continue to trump any existing or potential geopolitical strains.

The Euro-zone crisis erupted in Greece in the early months of 2009. By the early months of 2012, this apparently minor problem in the south-east periphery of the continent was threatening to sunder the Euro and potentially the EU. A global economic calamity dwarfing the post-Lehman experience seemed in serious prospect.

The now famous commitment by ECB President Mario Draghi in July 2012, in language reminiscent of a Clint Eastwood character, that "the ECB is ready to do whatever it takes to preserve the euro. And believe me, it will be enough", has dramatically reduced this threat. Bond investors and bank depositors in the Euro-zone are now as confident as their counterparts in the US, Japan or the UK that their central bank is effectively standing behind the liabilities of their member governments and banking systems.

Many respected commentators, such as Martin Wolf of the *Financial Times* speaking in Dublin recently, believe that this period of relative calm in the Euro-zone will likely give way to renewed turbulence at some stage. I am not particularly worried by this prospect. Again I could be wrong, but I believe the commitment by Draghi, crucially underwritten by Germany, effectively has removed the threat to the survival of the Euro, and that, for investors, the Euro-zone crisis is effectively over.

My greatest worry as an investor facing into the uncertain future is not geopolitical tensions, Euro-zone threats or any of a long list of other potential candidates.

My answer to the question at the PRMIA meeting and my greatest worry is that the crucial but nebulous glue of trust that holds our modern monetary and economic system together could come unstuck at any time. Indeed, I believe it very nearly did in the wake of the collapse of Lehman Brothers in 2008.

The success of policy-makers in piecing the humpty-dumpty of the financial system back together should not blind us to the unchanged risk at its heart, nor the potentially destabilising consequences of the extraordinary policy interventions still very much in place.

The warning of legendary investor Seth Klarman of Baupost, as he returned money to investors last autumn is timely:

> "Investing today may well be harder than it has been at any time in our three decades of existence, not because markets are falling but because they are rising; not because governments have failed to act but because they chronically overreact; not because we lack acumen or analytical tools but because the underpinnings of our economy and financial system are so precarious that the unabating risks of collapse dwarf all other factors".

The world changed on 15 August 1971. After almost a quarter of a millennium broadly tied to gold, the money of the world was cut free.

Since that dramatic night in the White House, we are all hostage to a compellingly-incentivised, rapidly-growing and bewilderingly-diverse money-creation machine. Moreover, the political and monetary authorities in whom we trust are little more than impotent accommodators of an unanchored monetary whirlwind beyond their control; a whirlwind, in truth, beyond any control.

When I ponder what to worry about, I start here.

46: BANKING INQUIRY GUARANTEED TO GIVE A SUMMER OF DRAMA AND ENTERTAINMENT

The Sunday Times, 29 June 2014

After much time and theatre, the Oireachtas banking enquiry is almost under way.

The death of Anglo, the birth of NAMA and the blanket liability guarantee are just some of the issues likely to be scrutinised by the inquiry in coming months. With the advent of this long-anticipated investigation, banking and banking-related matters are set to feature prominently in parliamentary debate after the summer recess.

To help prepare for this, the Office of the Oireachtas Library and Research Services recently tendered for a research paper on banking for TDs and Senators. It is to be between 3,000 and 4,500 words and "will be disseminated to members of the Oireachtas to enhance their understanding of the Irish banking system".

I have no idea how many papers have been tendered or by whom, but there are key aspects of banking that all our parliamentarians should ponder. This succinct insight by economist and diplomat John Kenneth Galbraith in 1975 is a good place to start:

> "The process by which banks create money is so simple that it repels the mind".

A man walks into a bank looking for a car loan of €10,000. The bank grants him the loan and credits his current account with €10,000. He gives a cheque drawn on his current account to the seller of the car and drives off to enjoy his new motoring experience.

The seller of the car lodges the cheque to his deposit account. If he uses the same bank as the car buyer, the bank now has a new asset in the form of the car loan, balanced by a new liability in the form of the seller's deposit account. If the seller uses another bank, the car buyer's bank will have his loan as an asset balanced by a liability in the form of an inter-bank loan from the seller's bank.

The bank profits from the difference in interest rates between what it receives on its assets and pays on its liabilities. The bank has a compelling incentive to repeat this process as often and in as big a size as possible.

The bank faces no effective constraint in exploiting this compelling incentive. The central bank is a passive accommodator of this money-creation power of the private banking system.

To the wry amusement of Galbraith, the money-creation process is that simple. Man looks for loan. Bank grants loan. Loan creates deposit. Borrower spends deposit. Bank pockets the difference between interest received on its loans and interest paid on its deposits.

It is hardly surprising that bank assets and liabilities – their balance sheets – have exploded since Nixon cut money free by abandoning the gold standard in 1971.

For example, although unchanged for centuries, in less than four decades in the run-up to the global financial crisis, bank balance sheets in the UK as a % of GDP exploded by a factor of five. In the less internationalised United States, this figure was still a stunning factor of three.

In Ireland, our need to adhere to an exchange rate target within the exchange rate mechanism of the EMS until 1999 meant our banks were delayed arrivals at the debt-creation party. However, they partied hard when it got there. In just six years from 2002 to 2008, lending by our so-called 'covered banks' almost trebled (see the chart below).

The fundamental point for our legislators to ponder is that private banks create most of our money out of thin air. The small amount of paper printed or coin minted is all but irrelevant. More than 97% of the money circulating today in leading economies such as the US, Japan or the Euro-zone has been loaned into existence by private banks.

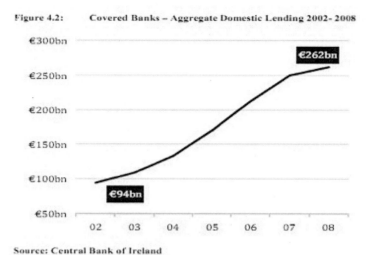

Figure 4.2:   Covered Banks – Aggregate Domestic Lending 2002- 2008

Source: Central Bank of Ireland

This money is invariably loaned to governments, households and corporations at interest rates higher than that paid on the liabilities created. On the assumption that their debtors pay them back, private banks have a compelling incentive to loan into existence as much money as possible.

Unfortunately, as we have experienced so painfully in Ireland, any doubts about the actual or perceived capacity of debtors to repay can cause widespread market, economic and social turmoil.

The long-awaited banking inquiry will likely provide much local colour on the collapse of the Irish banking system. The flawed decisions, personalities and regulations that fuelled our particular variant of boom, bubble and bust no doubt will provide much entertainment and spark much commentary.

In substance, though, our inquiry is unlikely to conclude much differently than long-serving Governor of the Bank of England, Mervyn King, speaking in New York in 2010:

> "Of all the many ways of organising banking, the worst is the one we have today".

47: INTELLIGENT INVESTORS CAN LOOK FORWARD TO A COMFORTABLE OLD AGE

The Sunday Times, 18 August 2014

In secondary school, my economics textbook outlined three distinct elements in explaining the role of money.

First, money acts as a unit of account, something that can be used to value goods and services, record debts, and make calculations. Drop into any shop in Ireland or across the Euro-zone and look at the goods on display. They will be priced in euros and cents. The role of money – in our case, the Euro – as a unit of account is clear, alive and well.

Second, money acts as a medium of exchange, something buyers can exchange with sellers when they want to purchase goods or services. You pay the quantity of euros and cents requested and you leave with the goods. The role of money as a medium of exchange is clear and ongoing.

Third, money acts as a store of value, something that can be used to transfer purchasing power from the present to the future. I believe, however, that it has become misleading to include this role in school textbooks or to use it as a credible guide for those with surplus euros — savers — who hope to store and grow their wealth. The global financial crisis has had many consequences. Of primary importance for the saver has been the extraordinary policy response of the main monetary authorities.

The US Federal Reserve, the Bank of England and the European Central Bank have followed the Bank of Japan by reducing the nominal risk-free returns on offer to sovereign bond investors and deposit account holders to historic lows. The likelihood of these rates returning to the 5% to 6% range of the past looks remote. This poses a stark challenge for savers hoping to store and grow their wealth. The crucial importance of the annual rate of return is powerfully illustrated by John Kay, a *Financial Times* commentator and author, in his book *The Long and the Short of It.*

"If you gathered nuts for your retirement for 25 years and planned to retire for 25 years, you would need to set aside half your nuts for old age," said Kay. "If you can earn a return on your savings, you can save much less." The table below shows how much less.

Save Now, Spend Later						
Annual rate of return	**10%**	**8%**	**6%**	**4%**	**2%**	**0%**
% of income required to save	8.5	12.7	19	27.3	37.9	50
% of income available to spend	91.5	87.3	81	72.7	62.1	50

The difference between achieving a 2% annual rate of return — roughly that offered by sovereign bonds and deposit accounts — and an 8% annual rate of return is striking. Kay makes a strong case that what he defines as "intelligent investors" can credibly expect to earn an after-tax annual rate of return of at least 8% on average over the long-term.

How can we heighten our probability of investing intelligently?

The first suggestion – euro cost averaging – is simple and mechanical. It aims to benefit from the inherent volatility of stock markets by investing regularly. The active value-investing approach of billionaire investor Warren Buffett and others who share his philosophy of investing in a portfolio of individually-analysed, sensibly-diversified and conservatively-valued assets has stood the test of time and logic. Followers of this approach generally invest in relatively-concentrated portfolios, where the top 20 to 25 holdings account for the bulk of their investment.

Nassim Taleb, an author and statistician, has been challenging many of the conventional underpinnings of financial market theory and behaviour since the publication of his provocative book *Fooled by Randomness* more than 10 years ago. Among much else in his latest book, *Antifragile*, I believe he makes a strong case for a different approach to intelligent investing to that followed and advocated by

Buffett. By embracing the futility of prediction and investing in a much more widely-diversified portfolio of assets, savers are increasing their exposure to rare, positive "black swans": exposures that pay off in a spectacularly positive, nonlinear fashion. Finally, the returns achieved should be further enhanced by having the discipline to tweak the mechanical application of euro cost averaging by investing more at times when the chosen portfolio is relatively "cheap" and *vice versa*.

Kay, Buffett, Taleb and others make compelling arguments for a more intelligent and rewarding approach. To store and grow our wealth in a way that money no longer can, it is in all our interests to start heeding them.

48: WHY A BOOMING STOCK MARKET CAN LEAVE INVESTORS IN DESPAIR

The Sunday Times, 31 August 2014

Standard and Poor's first published its widely-followed index of US shares, the S&P 500, on 4 March 1957. For the first time in 57 years, this index broke the 2,000 level last Monday, extending the remarkable rise under way since March 2009. If you invested €100 in this index at that time you would have almost €270 today – a gain of almost 170%.

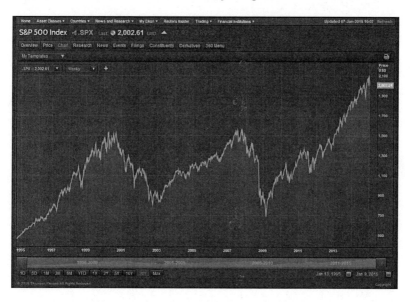

As news of the S&P 500's record highs was breaking, I happened to be in conversation with a friend who is an independent, fee-based financial adviser near Dublin. I assumed his clients would be pleased. On the contrary – many would be even more disillusioned with all things to do with investment, he said.

To give a flavour of this disillusion, he gave the example of a client who liquidated his pension investments in 2009 after they had fallen to

35% of their peak value two years earlier. The emotional pain of the loss and the fear of further loss had become too much to bear. Scarred by this experience, the fund has remained in cash since then and is consequently still hovering at about 35% of its peak value. For this investor, the surging stock market only rubs salt in the wound. According to my friend, this is a common story among Irish investors. He has encountered many who suffered heavy losses on property and bank shares and compounded the pain by their failure to regain any meaningful exposure to the recovery. Is it any wonder disillusion is so widespread among investors? My lazy assumption that rising stocks markets are good news for all could not have been wider of the mark.

This experience is by no means confined to Ireland.

Consider this comment from the *Credit Suisse Global Investment Returns Yearbook 2014*:

> "For the 20 years up to the end of 2013, the investor return in actively managed funds was just 60% to 80% of the return recorded by actively managed funds".

At first glance, it does not make sense that investors who own actively managed funds could earn returns lower than the funds themselves. The root of the problem is bad timing. Investors tend to extrapolate recent results. This pattern of investor behaviour is so consistent that academics have a name for it: the 'dumb money effect'. When markets are down investors are fearful and withdraw their cash. When markets are up they are greedy and add more cash.

This is not a new quirk of the human condition. The ancient Greeks grappled with the problem at the time of Homer. Before embarking on their epic Odyssey, the hero Odysseus and his crew were warned of the dangers, including the risks of shipwreck if they were lured by the sirens' call. To avoid temptation, Odysseus blocked his crew's ears. Homer knew precautions were needed to keep emotions in check.

The same insight holds true for modern investors seeking to avoid the 'dumb money effect'.

The simplest rule is to adhere to a buy and hold strategy. By binding themselves tightly to their initial exposure, ignoring the sirens' call to change tack in response to events, they stand a better chance of matching the returns of the funds in which they invest.

For those willing to bring a little more thought to the task, I believe an even better outcome is possible.

Ben Graham, widely acknowledged as the father of value investing, summarized his deceptively simple rules more than 80 years ago. Faithfully followed, I believe they still provide a compelling road map for the investor seeking a more rewarding answer than a buy and hold strategy.

> "A fundamental guiding rule is that the investor should never have less than 25% or more than 75% in common stocks, with a consequent inverse range of between 75% and 25% in bonds. There is an implication here that the standard division should be an equal one, or 50-50 between the two major investment mediums. However, the only investment principle that has ever worked well consistently is to buy common stocks at such times as they are cheap by analysis, and to sell them at such times as they are dear by analysis. That sounds like timing; but it is not really timing at all but rather the purchase and sale of securities by the method of valuation".

49: DRAGHI'S MOOTED MOVE ON QE OFFERS FRESH HOPE TO INVESTORS

The Sunday Times, 14 September 2014

Mario Draghi, the president of the European Central Bank (ECB), shows little sign of reversing his habit of confounding his many observers. His unexpected announcement on 4 September of a further cut in the main ECB policy interest rate to just 0.05% followed a series of unanticipated decisions by the former governor of the Bank of Italy since he took over the reins at the ECB in November 2011.

This latest easing of policy, bringing the policy rate to the brink of the zero-bound barrier, heightens the prospect of an even more radical direction in the period ahead.

ECB Policy Rate

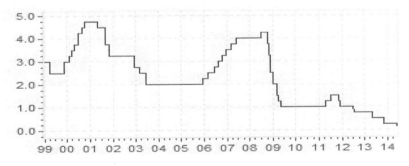

Source: ECB.

Although a man of surprises to date, it is increasingly likely that Draghi will follow his counterparts in Japan, the US and the UK by fully embracing quantitative easing (QE). It is timely to consider this often misunderstood policy and its implications for investors in more detail.

The common, but I believe mistaken, view is that QE is some sort of mechanical trigger that somehow 'floods' the banking system with 'money', sparking all sorts of supposedly obvious effects such as driving prices and/or economic activity higher.

In fact, QE is ultimately just the replacement of one (quasi-liquid) asset on bank balance sheets with another (purely liquid) asset. The central bank achieves this by buying the former from commercial banks with new reserves freshly created for the purpose.

The direct economic impact of this transaction is minimal. There was little prior constraint on the commercial bank making loans to credit-worthy borrowers that QE has magically removed. Little new spending, income or demand has been generated. The 'price' at which the asset purchase/sale happens may well be important if it serves to drive the general cost of money lower, but with money already so cheap across Europe and indeed the rest of the globe, the impact of this would be minimal.

The hard economic truth is that, in the absence of a fiscal expansion to directly generate new spending, income and demand, the trajectory of the Euro-zone economy is unlikely to be altered much by such monetary tinkering.

QE is better understood, not as a mechanical trigger, but as a psychological signal. Its impact was understandably greater therefore, when first signalled by the Federal Reserve and the BOE than in its later rounds. In particular, the implicit re-assurance signalled by the first round of QE in December 2008, that investors were not being completely abandoned to their fate as the financial crisis intensified, may well have played a decisive role in averting a re-run of the great depression of the 1930s. It should cement a positive place in history for the then Federal Reserve Chairman Bernanke, who had the courage and insight to embrace this unconventional tool in the face of widespread and often vitriolic criticism at that time.

The key signal for investors of an embrace of QE by the ECB is the likelihood of extremely low Euro-zone interest rates for a very long time. Extremely low rates are not a short-term aberration ahead of a return to 'normality', but the normality that is in prospect for the foreseeable future.

Draghi's latest intervention means investor thirst for income will be even more intense, and will remain difficult to sate for a very long time.

Predicting the direction of the general stock market is notoriously challenging. There are just too many variables. It is also important to remember that the absolute valuation of stocks is less attractive following the sharp rally of recent years.

However, many stocks continue to offer earnings – and in many cases dividend – yields well in excess of bond yields and deposit rates, suggesting a long period of very low rates remains far from the general expectation. This is the opportunity.

Investing in a portfolio of sensibly-diversified and conservatively-valued companies, as an alternative to leaving your money on deposit, is the key conclusion of Draghi's latest surprise. In this ongoing environment of meagre income, owning a share of good companies that offer this increasingly scarce return is the key message for investors of any QE signal from Frankfurt.

50: 'BANKING' AND 'CRISIS' – TWO SCARY WORDS THAT STILL SPOOK INVESTORS

The Sunday Times, 21 September 2014

The most popular property supplement in the country recently devoted half a page to the fortunes of a house in Drumcondra. The house was bought in the Spring of last year for €250,000 and transformed from a number of bedsits into a family residence, and is now for sale for €750,000. At the height of the property boom, houses like this changed hands for around €900,000. The physical transformation of this house may have been expensive and it may not sell for the asking price, but I think its price rebound captures well the rapid recovery of Dublin property.

In the main body of the same newspaper, readers were updated on the latest trek across Europe of Finance Minister Michael Noonan. In contrast to his predecessor, he is not looking to source funding from reluctant official creditors, but rather to convince those creditors to take their money back. Far from being beholden to the dreaded Troika for generations to come, it seems we now have to convince them to allow us to repay them. The irony is completed by noting that the funding to repay our official creditors will come from the private bond market, which is now mustard-keen to loan us as much as we want at historically low interest rates, having recoiled from loaning us anything at any price just a few short years ago.

With such welcome domestic developments and the accompanying talk of the end of austerity, it may seem churlish to raise a potential negative. However, I believe it's timely to be reminded that the global banking system remains a worrying threat. Indeed, it is still difficult to argue with the stark conclusion of then Bank of England Governor

Mervyn King in 2010 that "of all the many ways of organising banking, the worst is the one we have today".

Bank assets (mostly loans) are still supported by a relatively tiny sliver of equity, with the vast bulk still funded by debt. Moreover, there remains a massive mismatch between the generally long-term maturity of bank assets and the generally short-term maturity of bank debts. Almost uniquely therefore, banks are still businesses that cannot survive without the backing of central banks and ultimately governments.

In the context of the financial crisis and its aftermath, Barclays Bank often was cited as one of the 'good guys' because, in the words of its former boss Bob Diamond, it "didn't take a penny of taxpayers' money". However, this clearly missed the point that, without the implicit backing of the taxpayer, not to mention the explicit actions of the taxpayer elsewhere, Barclays would have imploded in 2008.

To get a sense of how little has changed since, consider the latest balance sheet for Barclays, as at the end of June this year.

Barclays Balance Sheet - End June 2014

Assets (£ Millions)		Liabilities (£ Millions)	
Loans & Other Assets	1,314,899	Liabilities	1,256,831
		Total Equity	58,068
Total	**1,314,899**	**Total**	**1,314,899**

The sliver of equity is still leveraged almost 23 times, meaning a fall of just 4% in the value of its assets would wipe it out. In addition, although not visible on the balance sheet here, the extent of the mismatch between the generally long-term maturity of its assets and the generally short-term maturity of its debts remains massive.

Barclays, like its banking counterparts across the globe, remains a business that cannot survive without the backing of its central bank and ultimately its government.

There is little reason to believe that the long association between the words 'banking' and 'crisis' is much looser today than before the crisis.

While this has many implications for public policy-makers, the key message for investors is that the risk borne by equity holders in a bank is of a fundamentally different order than that borne in almost any other business. This doesn't mean that there won't be periods when bank share prices rise, just that it is important not to invest in this possibility without considering the unusual nature of the risks involved. Banks remain a worry.

51: 'RISK-FREE' GERMAN BONDS MAY NOT BE FOOLPROOF FOR PENSIONS

The Sunday Times, 5 October 2014

Following a recent presentation to a group of pension trustees, a colleague was peppered with questions about the extraordinarily low level of current bond yields and the implications for the investment strategy. In particular, the trustees were keen to hear his views on the actuarial advice that, in order to reduce risk, the fund should be increasing its exposure to 'risk-free' German government bonds by reducing its exposure to 'risky' assets such as equities and property. A lively and important discussion ensued.

Pensions are generally a mass turn-off. The turgid language, perceived complexity and lack of immediate relevance make most people glaze over at the mere mention of how their retirement might be funded. Indeed, in recent years, the more pressing challenge of surviving the regular contractions in their income has seen many people relegate pensions even further down their list of priorities. However, the prospect that such income contraction may finally be drawing to a close may soon help to spark a greater engagement.

On the basis of the discussion sparked by the pension trustees above, such an engagement would be timely. The vast bulk of Irish pension assets are in defined benefit schemes where the risk that the assets prove insufficient to fund member benefits is borne by the employer. Defined benefit schemes across the economy are now being closed or amended in ways likely to disadvantage scheme members, because in calculating pension fund liabilities, actuaries base their calculation on a 'risk-free' rate sourced from the sovereign bond market.

In the Euro-zone, the yield on the 10-year German government bond is generally used as the appropriate 'risk-free' rate. With a negligible to zero probability of the German government failing to honour its promise to repay this bond in full and on time, the logic of using this yield as the 'risk-free' rate for such calculations seems to be unimpeachable.

I believe, however, it is crucial that pension fund members, trustees and public policy-makers challenge this assumption.

Following the collapse of Lehman Brothers in September 2008, the global economy and banking system faced collapse. Many feared a rerun of the Great Depression of the 1930s. This view failed to recognise the powerful levers available to policy-makers, which have been deployed with an aggression unprecedented in peace-time.

Of particular relevance to pensions, monetary policy-makers effectively have taken control of their government bond markets. Bond yields are now what the bureaucrats at the Federal Reserve, the BOE, the ECB and the BOJ determine them to be. Extraordinarily, nominal government bond yields out to 30 years are generally below the rate of inflation in most of these countries.

In the case of Germany, bond yields remain at incredibly low levels, hovering close to the lowest levels ever reached (see the graph below).

German 10-Year Bond Yield

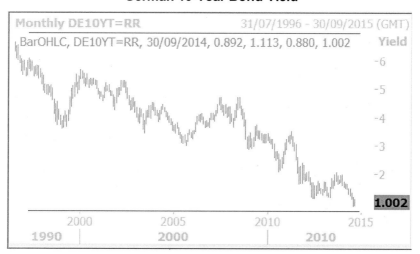

Source: Thompson Reuters.

The price to earnings (p/e) ratio is a relationship normally cited as a measure of value for equities. But as a tool for comparing the earnings of any asset, with the price of that asset, it can be usefully employed elsewhere. It is, after all, just the earnings yield inverted.

In the discussion with the pension trustees, my colleague used it in relation to the current German government 10-year bond. He pointed out that, at its current yield of 1%, this 'risk-free' asset is on a price to earnings ratio of 100 – a ratio similar to that of the Japanese and Nasdaq stock-markets at their peaks in 1989 and 2000 respectively. Described this way, the advice to increase exposure to German government bonds in order to reduce risk unsurprisingly lengthened the trustee meeting.

In a 2006 memo simply called 'Risk', renowned investor Howard Marks of Oaktree Capital sought to broaden the debate about investment risk from the actuarial and the conventional.

In an updated memo earlier this month, 'Risk Revisited', he returned to the fray with the crucial insight that:

> "Investors face two major risks: the risk of losing money and the risk of missing opportunities. Either can be eliminated but not both. And leaning too far in order to avoid one can set you up to be victimised by the other".

For pension scheme members, trustees and public policy-makers, it's time to take steps to avoid mechanically sleep-walking into such an outcome. To lessen this likelihood, replacing the current policy-distorted 'risk-free rate' in liability calculations by something like its 20-year average of around 4.25% should be urgently considered.

52: DAY TRADERS, LIKE MAFIA WIVES, ARE PLAYING A DANGEROUS GAME

The Sunday Times, 26 October 2014

For a while, the day-trader making easy money in the rising stock market of the late 1990s became a staple of popular culture. Most famously, the wife of fictional mafia boss Tony Soprano spent a few episodes of the classic TV series making more money out of trading technology shares than her husband was making out of his more traditional pursuits. In hindsight, the widespread lure to day trading of Mrs Soprano and others proved to be a good indicator that the market was heading for trouble.

So it proved. The Nasdaq peaked in March 2000 and collapsed by more than 80% over the next 30 months.

A recent BBC TV documentary on a new generation of day traders in the UK suggests that the lure of easy money is back. While not as widespread yet as in the heady days of Carmela Soprano and the Nasdaq, the stock-market advance of recent years seems to have sparked the return of the amateur trader ready to chance their luck and their money on the short-term vagaries of stock prices.

Before succumbing to the temptation to join them, it may be worth pondering an unchanging truth from Nassim Taleb in his best-selling book *Fooled by Randomness: The Hidden Role of Chance in Life and in the Markets*:

"Over a short time increment, one observes the variability of a portfolio, not the returns. When I see an investor monitoring his portfolio with live prices on his cellular telephone or his handheld, I smile and smile. The same methodology can explain why the news is full of noise and why it is better to read *The New*

Yorker on Mondays than *The Wall Street Journal* every morning (from the standpoint of frequency, aside from the massive gap of intellectual class between the two publications)".

By accepting this truth from Taleb, we should leave the day-traders to hope for the best in their frenzied pursuit of short-term profit.

Over the long-term, a share price is a function of the cash earnings distributed to shareholders. Simply put, as equity investors we should always remember that we are owners of a share in a business and that the value of the business to us is ultimately determined by the cash that we take out of it.

When a business makes a profit, it has two options for deploying it:

- Re-invest it – in either the existing business, or by acquiring all or part of a new one;
- Distribute it to shareholders – in either a dividend, or by buying back and cancelling some outstanding shares.

Ideally, as shareholders we want the management of the business to take the first option up to the point where it generates a positive net present value to us, and to take the second option with the residual.

However, in the real world, even the most appropriately motivated and incentivised management team will find it impossible to live up to this ideal. There are just too many variables outside their control.

The best that we can reasonably hope for is a sensible combination of the two. From the businesses in which we own shares therefore, we should demand capable management to generally generate profit, re-invest or acquire profitably for the future, and/or pay-out a steady stream of income to us.

Framed in this way, it should be clear why dividends and earnings are highly correlated over time. The former is just a greater or lesser, but fundamentally more stable, sub-set of the latter.

Curiously, many investors eschew this framework and narrowly think of dividends purely as a source of income rather than a function of profitability. They often think of dividends as a sign that growth is slowing down.

In reality, a large diversity of businesses both pay and grow dividends. Many of these are enjoying profit growth in excess of the opportunities to re-invest profitably. More generally, companies that can sustain higher dividends tend to be more profitable and those that cannot tend to be under pressure. This is the opportunity.

Across a portfolio and over time, studying the dividend pattern and investing accordingly can help to tilt the probability in favour of choosing sustainably more profitable businesses and avoiding their less profitable counterparts. This is an approach to making money from the stock market much more likely to succeed than day trading short-term noise. A lesson just as relevant to investors today as to the wife of a fabled mafia don in the glory days of the technology bubble.

53: NO 'HAPPY EVER AFTER' IF YOU LISTEN TO FINANCIAL MARKET FAIRY TALES

The Sunday Times, 2 November 2014

We all love stories. From the bedtime stories of our early childhood to the novels, films and dramas that dominate much of our popular culture, our widespread need for narrative has deep and enduring roots. We need stories to simplify and digest the often bewildering complexity of much that confronts us.

In many areas of life, this is generally a positive. Sports-fans, cinema-goers and history-buffs, to name just three, all derive great satisfaction from engrossing themselves in the twisting narratives of their favourite teams, films or historical stories. Little harm and often much joy, results from such activity.

Unfortunately, our addiction to stories is not always so benign.

Recent years have seen every twist and turn of the stock, bond or currency markets become a staple segment of traditional television news broadcasts, not to mention the proliferation of channels and websites that are now devoted to dissecting every blip across the financial market landscape.

Investors, traders and the general public seem to have an insatiable need for narratives to help them make sense of the dizzying and constantly moving array of financial market prices that ceaselessly confront them. These narratives in turn are provided by a large army of commentators, analysts, strategists and assorted others, who soothingly connect cause and effect for their grateful audiences.

One danger of this for our pocket is captured by psychologist and Nobel Laureate in Economics, Daniel Kahneman, in his insight on our strong tendency to 'anchor'. We have a strong and enduring bias to allow an initial piece of information, interpretation or story to dominate our decision-making. Subsequent information is interpreted in this context rather than objectively, thereby heightening our likelihood of making poor decisions.

Kahneman regularly cites the example of the Bloomberg news reports on stock market movement on the day that Saddam Hussein was captured. According to Bloomberg, both the morning market rally and the afternoon collapse were caused by the capture of the former Iraqi dictator. The anchored belief that news on the fate of Saddam Hussein must cause the stock market to move proved so strong that Bloomberg attributed both the *rise* and the *fall* of the market that day to the same event.

As investors, while this is clearly a bias that we must be alive to in ourselves, it is also impacting the stories we are being told by the army of 'talking heads' across the media in ways impossible for us to interpret. Contrary to our instincts and suppressing our need for narrative, ignoring these stories and the story-tellers is likely to be a profitable decision.

In related fashion, following a series of recent meetings with existing and prospective investors, I was struck by how often we were asked the question of how much time we devote to meeting the management of the companies in which we own shares, or are considering owning shares.

Many of these investors and prospective investors were clearly of the view that meeting management and hearing their story is an important part of an investment process. They had been bolstered in this by many investment managers who had outlined to them how it plays a key role in their investment decision-making.

In this context, our answer that we never met the management of the companies in which we own shares or are considering owning shares unsurprisingly sparked some lively debates. An old example proved helpful.

Some years ago, a colleague of mine was working on a research report on the US toy company Mattel. At the time, like many investment managers to this day, we believed in the benefit of meeting company management and hearing their story if at all possible. Consequently, we were more than happy to accept a broker invitation to meet the then CEO of Mattel as he passed through Dublin on an investor road-show.

The share price had been under pressure as the company toy offerings were losing ground to competitors. The impressive CEO told us a convincing story of how the upcoming Christmas season would see a resurgence of demand focussed on their new range of toys. We bought the shares.

Unfortunately, his confidently narrated belief in a positive Christmas season proved to be wide of the mark. The share price continued to fall and it proved to be a poor investment.

There were many lessons to be drawn from this experience – not least the futility of trying to predict the Christmas preferences of millions of children!

More generally, as an investor or potential investor, the danger in meeting company managements and hearing their stories is rooted in the 'anchoring' bias. Even with an awareness of the risk, we are likely to be anchored in our thinking and decision-making by an impressive company management with a compelling story. A danger best and easily avoided.

The enjoyment of stories is a deep-rooted part of being human. Changing that is not an option and nor should we want it to be, but we should be extremely careful of the domains in which we indulge it. Listening to the often beguiling stories of market pundits or company managements should not be among them.

54: STRESS TESTS FAIL TO SOLVE THE PROBLEM OF BANKS' VULNERABILITY

The Sunday Times, 30 November 2014

Media coverage of the recently completed stress tests of Euro-zone banks has been extensive, and the financial cost has been substantial. In Ireland alone, the eight banks covered in the tests paid more than €17m for the privilege.

Unfortunately, both the coverage and the cost were a waste of time and money. In terms of reassuring investors and tax-payers that these banks have been reformed successfully and are no longer a major economic threat, the tests were little more than a costly charade.

Banks remain structurally vulnerable to crisis. We cannot know when or where the next banking crisis will erupt, but we do know that, with the banks' current structure, there will be one. The stress tests do nothing to change this.

The then Governor of the Bank of England, Sir Mervyn King summarised this memorably at a speech in New York in 2010, 'Banking – from Bagehot to Basel and Back Again':

> "Banking crises are endemic to the market economy that has evolved since the Industrial Revolution. The words 'banking' and 'crisis' are natural bedfellows. If love and marriage go together like a horse and carriage, then banking and crisis go together like Oxford and the Isis, intertwined for as long as anyone can remember".

The fundamental difference between banks and other businesses is their capital structure. In comparison to almost any other business, banks remain overwhelmingly financed by debt.

This has not always been the case, but has become their defining feature over the past few decades.

For example, although unchanged for centuries, in less than four decades in the run-up to the global financial crisis bank balance sheets in the UK as a % of GDP – overwhelmingly funded by money owed to depositors, bondholders and each other – exploded by a factor greater than five (see the graph below).

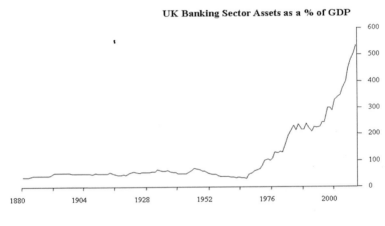

UK Banking Sector Assets as a % of GDP

Source: Bank of England.

The following comment by King from the same speech in 2010 captures this changed reality well:

> "While banks' balance sheets have exploded, so have the risks associated with those balance sheets. Capital ratios have declined and leverage has risen. The size, concentration and riskiness of banks have increased in an extraordinary fashion and would be unrecognisable to Bagehot".

Simply put, in a relatively short period of time, banks have exploded into highly-leveraged, challengingly-complex, intricately-connected and systemically-important giants looming over the global economy.

Despite the widespread commitment to reform in the wake of the financial crisis and the various measures put in train since, banks remain fundamentally unchanged. More specifically, the much trumpeted stress tests give us no reason to believe that the long association between the words 'banking' and 'crisis' is much looser today than before the crisis.

The sliver of equity in Euro-zone banks is still leveraged around 23 times - a fall of just 4% in the value of bank assets will likely push us back into 'bail-out territory'. As the assets of the bankrupt Anglo Irish Bank and Irish Nationwide Building Society collapsed by around 40% in the crisis, there is scant comfort in such a thin buffer.

For investors and tax-payers, the pain of the financial crisis may be lessening with time. However, far from marking a watershed allowing us to move on from the banking catastrophe, the recent stress test charade should alert us to the threat that remains from our fundamentally-unchanged and structurally-fragile banking system. In short, banks remain vulnerable.

55: A WINNING PORTFOLIO IS A DIVERSIFIED ONE

The Sunday Times, 14 December 2014

John Kenneth Galbraith, the influential economist, provided timeless wisdom and a clear challenge to active investors when he said:

> "There are two types of forecasters – those who don't know and those who don't know they don't know".

In grappling with such acumen, the philosopher and author Nassim Nicholas Taleb provides us with the following nugget in his best-known work, *The Black Swan: The Impact of the Highly Improbable*:

> "Knowing that you cannot predict does not mean that you cannot benefit from unpredictability".

Distilling these insights, the challenge for active investors is to shape portfolios that do not depend on views of the future portfolios that are protected from potentially bad news while simultaneously positioned to benefit from potentially good news. Or, simply put, to beat the market by benefiting from unpredictability.

The necessity of diversification is unarguable. However, many investors see it as a necessary evil that provides some comfort on the downside at the price of diluting potential returns on the upside. This may be true for a thoughtlessly applied approach to diversification. Investors should not fear sacrificing returns, though, if they employ a more tailored approach, grounded in a thoughtfully credible investment philosophy.

Indeed, such a thoughtfully tailored approach to diversification can combine the usual benefits of downside comfort with the upside benefit of exposure to lots of potentially positive news — in other words, a portfolio benefiting from unpredictability.

The potential for such an attractive combination is powerfully illustrated by considering the returns of the 24 MSCI global industry groups over the past three years.

Returns ranged from a loss of 1.9% for materials to a gain of 88.3% for media.

Many investors spend a great deal of time trying to position their exposure across these industry groups, hoping to capture relative performance changes between them. To enhance potential returns, these investors are consciously reducing their relative diversification. They are adhering to the conventional perspective that, in order to enhance upside potential, the trade-off must be a more concentrated exposure.

However, the dispersion of returns within the 24 industry groups over the period was significantly greater than the differences in returns between them. That is, the performance difference between the best and worst stocks in each industry group was much greater than the difference between the top-performing group (media) and the worst performer (materials).

Consider the North American technology sector. It performed well, gaining 60% over the three years. Within this category, however, there was a difference of 461% between the worst performing stock, BlackBerry, which lost more than half its value, and the best performer, Seagate, which gained more than 400% (see graph).

The huge dispersion of returns within each of the industry groups confirms that the expected trade-off between upside potential and diversification/concentration has no basis in fact.

Even more tantalisingly, this dispersion raises the real possibility of the opposite being the case: potential upside is enhanced as diversification is increased. The opportunity to tilt exposure towards the 'winners' and away from the 'losers' is improved by having as wide a diversity of exposures as possible across the global industry groups. Reducing diversification reduces this opportunity.

The consequent approach is to embrace the opportunity of such diversification by owning a large number of stocks, spread across a large number of regions and industries that have been chosen for their better likelihood than their peers of benefiting from good news or not suffering from bad news.

Industry: North America Technology: Relative performance, 3 years to 30 June 2014

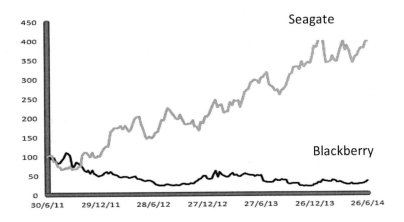

Source: Kleinwort Benson Investors.

Such a portfolio would possess the very desirable characteristics of facing into the unknowable future tailored to benefit both from the unpredictable and the passage of time. A portfolio shaped to have a large number of small and tailored risks, rather than one with a small number of large ones. The only prediction involved is that both Galbraith and Taleb would likely approve.

56: THERE'S NO SUCH THING AS A DEAD CERT

The Sunday Business Post, 4 January 2015

Driving to visit my parents some years ago, I stopped to fill up at a busy, suburban petrol station. At the time, the oil price had been rising sharply and the airwaves were thick with earnest babble about the many implications flowing from sharply rising energy costs.

Just as I replaced the petrol cap on my car, I was approached by a well-known radio broadcaster wielding a microphone. He explained that he was recording a voxpop for broadcast later that day and enquired if he could ask me a few questions.

The conversation went something like this:

Q: *Given the reality of 'peak oil' and the inevitable rise in oil prices and energy costs, how do you expect to change your behaviour?*

A: *I would be wary of assuming anything about the oil price, and wary about changing my behaviour based on anything as uncertain as the oil price.*

Q: *What? Surely you know that the world is running out of oil and that the oil price will inevitably keep rising?*

A: *I don't know that, and while you may well be right, there is no way that you can know it either.*

At this point, he switched off his microphone, muttered something about not having time to waste on ignorant people, and headed across the forecourt to engage with a more worthwhile interviewee. Needless to say, his brief exchange with me did not make the evening broadcast.

I was reminded of this experience just before Christmas when we received an urgent client request for our investment outlook following the recent collapse in the oil price and the related market turmoil in Russia. My reply was a little pointed and consequently was softened a little by one of my colleagues before dispatch, but I think the original is worth sharing:

> "We have no strong convictions about either the outlook for oil prices and/or the outlook for Russia. Indeed, the very dramatic recent events in both, underlines for us the foolishness and often investment danger of holding such convictions.
>
> By contrast, our conviction that constructing broadly diversified portfolios with a strong dividend, quality and value orientation enhances our chances of harvesting alpha over the long-term is strengthened by such unpredictable events.
>
> While we accept that you are likely to receive many opinions on what we believe are the 'unknown, unknowns' of recent events, and how they may evolve from here, we hope you understand why we see little value in adding to them".

The lessons from this experience apply well beyond the oil market or Russia. With the sound of competing certainties from the large army of investment gurus louder than ever at this time of year, it may be more than usually important to heed some of them:

- There are no investment certainties;
- The game is about possibilities and probabilities, not right and wrong;
- The necessity of diversification is unarguable;
- Sticking to a credible process for tilting the likelihood of success in your favour is the best that you or your investment manager can hope to do;
- All else is thinly or elaborately disguised guesswork.

Over the last decade, the oil price has more than doubled, more than halved, more than doubled again and more than halved again, in a random path of unknowable direction (see the graph below).

Brent Crude Oil – 10-Year Chart

Source: Thompson Reuters.

For all of that period, investors have been bombarded by the certain pronouncements of countless experts on where the oil price or indeed any other financial variable is inevitably going. Like my radio interviewer at the petrol station, such experts usually offer a plausible sounding reason for their confident conviction.

As we face into the New Year, my only advice is to steer well clear of such certainties. They may be interesting and even entertaining at times, but are also likely to be costly.

57: DON'T TRY BEATING THE MARKETS, UNLESS YOU ARE WARREN BUFFETT

The Sunday Times, 11 January 2015

The dominant orthodoxy in finance over the past 60 years has been the efficient market hypothesis (EMH). Developed in the early 1950s by a varied group of US academics, some of whom received Nobel prizes for their efforts, the key conclusion is that trying to beat financial markets is a fool's errand.

Market prices jiggle about randomly, discounting all new information almost instantaneously, rendering it impossible to beat the market. In the face of this conclusion, rational investors should eschew any attempt to beat the market, relying instead on relatively low-cost passive vehicles that merely mimic the markets. The explosive growth of such vehicles, pioneered by John Bogle at Vanguard in the US in the early 1970s and subsequently spread across the financial world, is testament to the powerful and enduring influence of the EMH. Nevertheless, the EMH has shown sufficient flaws to suggest that attempting to beat the market may not always be a foolhardy endeavour.

There are inefficiencies in the behaviour of market economies and the financial markets embedded within them, which the active investor with the right approach may have an attractive probability of exploiting. In the wake of the global financial crisis of recent years, the need for more realistic frameworks to help understand the behaviour of economies and markets has become acute. For example, the financial instability hypothesis published in 1975 by Hyman Minsky, a long-neglected US economist, has returned to the fore as a more plausible description of how a dynamic market economy behaves in practice.

Minsky's characterisation of the market economy as a system   prone to bouts of dramatic instability generated endogenously by the financial system chimed well in the dramatic days up to and after the collapse of Lehman Brothers. The key insight that stability can lead to instability credibly captured the post-Cold War experience and its shuddering denouement. By contrast, the equilibrium-seeking system of orthodox theory, where instability is impossible, has been exposed as a flawed framework dangerously divorced from reality. In like fashion, the fallibility of the EMH has been laid bare.

A broad range of research in the area of behavioural economics and finance has shaken the hypotheses. In a recent speech on herd behaviour and keeping up with the Joneses, the economist Andrew Oswald outlined how individual rationality can often be consistent with collective catastrophe. Taking his lead from the animal kingdom, Oswald argues that humans are frightened of falling behind and are consequently prompted to constantly adjust their relative position within a group just as an animal seeking safety will do in a herd. As with the herd, however, individually rational behaviour on can occasion lead to collective catastrophe. The stark image of sheep plunging to their deaths in Thomas Hardy's *Far From the Madding Crowd*, following each other over the cliff to maintain their relative position, has clear real-world implications.

The shock of this realisation was famously expressed by long-time advocate of economic and finance orthodoxy Alan Greenspan, who told a US congressional committee in October 2008:

> "Yes, I've found a flaw [in my ideology]. I don't know how significant or permanent it is. But I've been very distressed by that fact. The modern risk management paradigm held sway for decades. The whole intellectual edifice, however, collapsed in the summer of last year and the crisis has turned out to be much broader than anything I could have imagined".

The famous investor Warren Buffett has spent recent years vying with his good friend Bill Gates for top spot in the *Fortune 500* list of the wealthiest people on the planet. If Buffett were the sole success of value-oriented investing, it would be difficult to disagree with the EMH.

However, in addition to the remarkable success of Buffett, there is a substantial body of evidence to suggest a value-oriented approach to investing has been consistently successful in beating the market.

Seth Klarman of Baupost, a hedge fund, pointedly grounds the success of value-oriented investing in the delusion of market efficiency:

> "Despite the comfortable academic consensus of market efficiency, financial markets will never be efficient because markets are, and will always be, driven by human emotion: greed and fear. Markets, and the prices of individual securities, will periodically and unpredictably overshoot. Also, skills and time horizons of market participants will obviously vary. Academics are deliberately blind to the 50-plus year track record of Buffett as well as those of other accomplished investors for, if markets are efficient, how can their astonishing success possibly be explained?".

58: NATIONAL SOVEREIGNTY IS REDUNDANT IN THE MODERN WORLD

The Sunday Business Post, 11 January 2015

A sense of 'sovereignty lost' pervaded much of the debate here during the troika years. Equated closely in the public mind with our dependence on funding from the IMF, EU and ECB, it is not surprising that the government and many commentators argued that a key motivation for striving to successfully exit our programme was that 'sovereignty' would be restored. Equally, many of the arguments of those who opposed the programme implied that its rejection would have been akin to throwing off the yoke of external oversight and would have represented a bold reassertion of this 'lost' ideal.

This often emotive issue also seems to have driven much of the soul-searching about the crisis in Spain and Italy. The Spanish government showed great reluctance to suffer the perceived diminution of 'sovereignty' of entering a programme comparable to Greece, Ireland and Portugal, while many believe that Italy would have somehow chosen to re-embrace the lira rather than suffer such a perceived affront to their 'sovereign' pride.

These arguments are mired in a timewarp. It is as if we have travelled back to the thinking of the late 19th or early 20th century and are now unable or unwilling to draw on the lessons of the century since. The newly-elected Irish government of March 1932 took office with the clear purpose of asserting our 'sovereignty' across as many areas as possible. In the economic sphere, this assertion took the form of a committed protectionism as we embarked on nearly three decades of economically turning our back on the rest of the world. Safely ensconced behind protective tariffs, we sought to produce sufficient output to satisfy domestic demand. The policy goal was to be free to make our own national decisions, encumbered by as few outside entanglements as possible. The result was a social and economic cataclysm. Most poignantly, a stagnant economy drove many hundreds of thousands of ill-prepared people to emigrate. The assertion of 'sovereignty' via a policy of protectionism was also a disaster for the great majority of those who stayed behind. It lead to such despair that some began to question the very viability of the state itself. They began to wonder if a return to the United Kingdom, if possible, might be the best option for the wellbeing of future generations. The irony of pursuing a policy purporting to assert 'sovereignty' while almost destroying it would be amusing if it hadn't been so destructive.

The coming to power of Sean Lemass in 1959 finally saw the reversal of this failed approach. Inspired by the ideas of TK Whitaker, a new political and economic policy actively sought engagement with the outside world. Trade barriers were gradually dismantled, foreign direct investment encouraged and we began the steady march towards sharing a market, a currency and a political framework with our European neighbours. The contrast with what went before could hardly have been more complete. The subsequent transition from being a basic producer of bulk agricultural product, dependent on the often volatile British market, to being a broad-based, service economy exporting across the globe has been a spectacularly positive one.

Today, in one of the most open economies in the world, the idea that being free to set tariff barriers could offer us a path to prosperity seems as misguided as much else from the often strange maelstrom of thinking which characterised the 'hungry 30s'. A favoured assertion of 'sovereignty' by Irish governments in more recent decades has been in the fiscal sphere. While not as destructive in human terms as the protectionist experiment from the 30s to the 60s, this assertion of 'sovereignty' has nonetheless driven the state to the brink of bankruptcy twice over the past 30 years. Fundamentally, the compulsion to make inflexible spending commitments with ephemeral revenue flows has proven dangerously addictive to our political system. We are still living through the wrenching aftermath of the most recent episode. By dominating, in particular, the half-decade until the financial and economic implosion of 2008, this addiction ultimately left our economy and society weak, bitter and confused.

Before Lemass and Whitaker, we learned the hard way that there was no sustainable prosperity in playing around with trade barriers. More recently, we have also learned that there is no sustainable prosperity in running unsustainable fiscal deficits. The exercise of illusionary 'sovereignty' via such policies has done us much harm. The continued peddling of these and related illusions about our 'sovereign' power has the potential to do us much more. As our political system fragments and the drumbeat of competing political promises grow louder, we need to stop seeking succour in dangerous illusions. More specifically, with the growing likelihood of our fellow EU citizens in Greece succumbing to the risky allure of such thinking, we should have learned enough from our own history to resist the empty temptation to follow them. The time for indulging the politics of tantrum and illusion is running out.

59: SWISS DISH OUT TRADERS A DOSE OF COLD TURKEY

The Sunday Times, 25 January 2015

Switzerland prides itself on stability. In contrast with many of its neighbours, the Alpine nation's neutrality and long history of prosperous engagement with the outside world have seen its citizens enjoy many years of political and economic calm. On any list of countries likely to be embroiled in financial market turmoil, comfortable and careful Switzerland is traditionally at or near the bottom.

This all changed on Thursday, 15 January. The decision of the Swiss National Bank (SNB) to remove the cap on the exchange rate between the Euro and the Swiss franc caused widespread market turmoil, with the franc appreciating by 16% against Europe's single currency.

The reaction of trader Rocky Muddar at TradeNext gives a good flavour of the impact:

> "15/1/15 will be remembered for many years as a day that ended many a trader's career and saw the collapse of numerous financial institutions and hedge funds. As someone who has traded the most volatile interest rate and bond futures, I have never seen such a swift and aggressive move in a major financial market like this in my life".

The view from the trading room was echoed in the halls of academia. Keith Pilbeam, professor of international economics at City University London, said the move caught many traders and hedge funds off guard. "We have not seen a day like this in the foreign exchange market for over 20 years, and many people have been caught completely by surprise", he said.

As is usual after such an event, the airwaves were soon thick with voices purporting to explain it. For example, many pundits spoke of expected quantitative easing by the European Central Bank (ECB) as the likely trigger for the Swiss surprise. Others asserted the move was inevitable, regardless of what the ECB decided in the face of ongoing capital flows into the Switzerland.

Maybe these explanations are of some benefit. However, I think the real lesson for investors has nothing to do with Switzerland, the SNB, the Swiss franc or the ECB.

The real lesson of 15 January is that the 'Taleb Turkey' returned with his usual vengeance to wreak havoc on those who had forgotten him.

In his classic article, 'The Fourth Quadrant: A Map of the Limits of Statistics', the philosopher and trader Nassim Taleb tells a tale with clear relevance to the decision by the SNB and its chaotic aftermath:

> "A turkey is fed for 1000 days – every day confirms to its statistical department that the human race cares about its welfare 'with increased statistical significance'. On the 1001st day, the turkey has a surprise".

Unfortunately, turkeys don't just come in the feathered variety. Lulled into similar complacency as the Taleb turkey, many traders and investors have lost heavily because of the SNB's actions. The history of such episodes seems of little value in dissuading fresh victims.

To avoid the fate of the turkey, investors should remember:

- Prediction is futile;
- There are no investment certainties;
- The game is about possibilities and probabilities, not right and wrong;
- The necessity of diversification is unarguable;
- Sticking to a credible process for tilting the likelihood of success in your favour is the best that you can hope to do;
- All else is thinly or elaborately disguised guesswork.

60: GERMAN ORTHODOXY HAS LOST OUT TO PRACTICAL POLITICS

The Sunday Business Post, 25 January 2015

The governing council of a central bank, like its political or religious equivalent, is always keen to display unity in public. The authority and credibility of the institution and its policies are generally viewed as sacrosanct. Particularly on issues that give rise to intense internal debate, the unwritten rule of rallying around a common policy for external consumption is seldom broken.

The very public disagreement therefore, between the president of the European Central Bank (ECB), Mario Draghi, and the president of the Bundesbank, Jens Weidmann, over the current direction of ECB policy is both unusual and significant.

This breach has been on clear public display since the decision by Weidmann over two years ago to draw a barely veiled equivalence between his nominal superior at the ECB and the gullible Emperor unwittingly tempted into "money-printing" disaster by Mephistopheles in the second part of Faust.

Such a public display of disagreement and the choice of such a disparaging fictional parallel pointedly highlight the extent of the chasm.

Facing into a decisive period in the high stakes challenge of tacking deflation in the Eurozone, the outcome of this conflict at the governing council is of potentially historic import. It is little exaggeration to suggest that the future of the Eurozone, and with it that of the global economy, are now being fought over in Frankfurt. A more important contemporary clash is difficult to imagine.

At its heart, this conflict is between the strict monetary orthodoxy of Weidmann and the more nuanced policy of conditional market intervention, popularly known as quantitative easing (QE), favoured by Draghi.

Difficult as it may seem in the current environment, Weidmann is concerned about the potential effect of such an ECB intervention on inflationary expectations, a concern with particular historic resonance for his native Germany.

Even more fundamentally, his deep-seated fear of any move towards central bank financing of governments has made him an implacable opponent of Draghi.

The unification of Germany in 1990 was one of the most significant political events and economic events since the end of World War II. Little more than four decades after a defeated, impoverished and despised country had been divided by its enemies, a democratic colossus at the heart of Europe was formed in peace amid general international goodwill.

While this development may look natural in hindsight, it was by no means inevitable that the collapse of Soviet power would be followed by German unification. Indeed, the probability of such an outcome could not have been high in the face of the many historic, geopolitical and economic obstacles confronting Chancellor Helmut Kohl in those heady days of 1989/1990.

The economic challenges alone looked daunting. For most economists, the joining together of as wealthy and dynamic market economy with its poor and stagnant centrally-planned neighbour was something that would take decades. Whatever political arrangements were to be agreed, economic rationality would demand that the path to German economic and monetary union would have to be a slow one.

This was certainly the view of the widely-respected president of the Bundesbank at the time, Karl-Otto Pohl, who in his 11th year at the helm of the powerful Frankfurt institution was probably the most-renowned central banker in the world.

His desire that economic rationality trump political aspiration in guiding policy crystallised around the issue of the exchange rate on union between the deutschmark and the ostmark.

Economics demanded that the ostmark be valued at a fraction of the deutschmark. Politics, and above all the need to maintain the positive momentum towards the union of East and West, demanded that each ostmark be valued as a deutschmark.

Helmut Kohl made the historic choice demanded by politics. Each ostmark was exchanged for a deutschmark, and Germany was unified. Pohl, the longstanding and widely-respected president of the Bundesbank, effectively was forced to fall on his sword.

No two battles are exactly comparable, but the current one between the monetary orthodoxy of Bundesbank president Weidmann and the more nuanced approach of ECB president Draghi has strong echoes of the Pohl-Kohl clash in 1990.

Expect politics to triumph again. The greater practical fear of the euro breaking up will trump the more theoretical fears of Weidmann.

The decision on Thursday by the ECB to follow its counterparts in the US, Britain and Japan by embarking on a large-scale bond purchasing programme is a further battle won by Draghi. Whatever fresh challenges emerge from Athens or elsewhere in the coming weeks, politics demands that the necessary compromises will be found.

Before drawing any more fictional parallels about Signor Draghi, Herr Weidmann might be better advised to remember the fate of his illustrious but ultimately defeated predecessor at the Bundesbank.

ABOUT THE AUTHOR

John Looby has been grappling with financial markets for almost a quarter of a century. In roles spanning fixed income, absolute return and equities, his fascination with the challenge of trying to beat the market has never dimmed. In more recent times, he has become particularly interested in the interplay between active investing and the ideas of author and philosopher Nassim Nicholas Taleb. He is currently a portfolio manager on the global equity team at Kleinwort Benson Investors in Dublin and a board member of the Value Investment Institute (**www.valueinstitute.org**). All of the opinions expressed in this collection are his own.

ABOUT OAK TREE PRESS

Oak Tree Press develops and delivers information, advice and resources for entrepreneurs and managers. It is Ireland's leading business book publisher, with an unrivalled reputation for quality titles across business, management, human resources, law, marketing and enterprise topics.

NuBooks is its recently-launched imprint, publishing short, focused ebooks for busy entrepreneurs and managers.

Oak Tree Press is comfortable across a range of communication media – print, web and training, focusing always on the effective communication of business information.

Oak Tree Press, 19 Rutland Street, Cork, Ireland.

T: + 353 21 4313855 F: + 353 21 4313496.

E: info@oaktreepress.com

W: www.oaktreepress.com / www.SuccessStore.com.